HANDWRITING LINK

An evidence-based approach to an integrated literacy program

Year 1 Workbook Teacher's Handbook

Carol A. Christensen and Glenn A. Christensen

Production staff
Graphics/Layout: Dean Maynard
Publisher: Rob Watts

Knowledge Books and Software
ABN 75003053316
PO Box 50, Sandgate, Queensland 4017
Phone: (07) 5568 0288
Fax: (07) 5568 0277
Email: orders@kbs.com.au
Website: www.kbs.com.au

Printed in Australia

Product code: E540

ISBN: 9781921016059

Table of Contents

Blank page intentionally added.

Background to the Program

The Role of Handwriting in Production of High Quality Written Text.

There is a remarkably strong relationship between handwriting and the quality of written text that children can produce. Research shows that for students from Prep to Year 10, handwriting has a greater impact on measures of quality of text than all other factors combined. Remarkably, between 50% and 65% of the difference between students in terms of the quality of their written text is due to differences in proficiency in handwriting.

Measures of quality of written text assess factors such as the creativity and originality of ideas, logical organisation and structuring of ideas, comprehensive presentation of arguments, sensitivity to the reader and communicative competence and technical accuracy of skills such as spelling and grammar. Research shows that handwriting has a dramatic impact on these diverse competencies. In other words, handwriting is a critically important skill in enabling students to produce text that is highly original and creative, logically organised and technically accurate.

It is perhaps counter-intuitive to suggest that handwriting has an impact on students' ability to produce high quality written text. For many years handwriting was seen as a low-level, technical skill and consequently of relatively little importance in developing higher-order competencies. However, both theory and research support the idea that proficiency in handwriting is essential to the production of text.

The impact of handwriting on written language relates primarily to the way in which the human mind works. In order to undertake any complex intellectual task, an individual must focus attention on the task. However, individuals are severely limited in their access to attentional resources. In fact, an individual has only sufficient attention to focus on one conscious intellectual activity at a time. Creating written text requires the execution of many attention-demanding activities. For example, writers must think about the ideas that they are going to include in their text. They also need to think about how they are going to organise, sequence and structure the presentation of their ideas. Selection of vocabulary and technical accuracy of spelling and grammar also need to be considered. In addition, writers should produce text that is appropriate for a particular audience and strive to create text that is clear and easy for the reader to follow. Because of the attentional limitations of the human mind, writers cannot think of all of these things at the same time.

One way of addressing this problem is to sequence attention-demanding tasks. Many of the tasks required in writing can be sequenced, so that writers focus attention on only one activity at a time. Producing multiple drafts can achieve this so that writers focus attention on one task in the first draft and then focus attention on another task in a subsequent draft. For example, a writer may focus attention on capturing interesting, creative ideas in their first draft. In subsequent drafts they might think about organising ideas, communicative clarity and technical accuracy. In this way, writers can focus attention on the tasks that require attention, but only attend to one task at a time.

Unfortunately, in some cases different processes must be executed simultaneously. Writers cannot address attentional demands of handwriting by using multiple drafts. Handwriting is an area where writers must generate letters and words at the same time that they are thinking about the content of their text. If writers focus attention on handwriting, then they do not have attention available for the most complex and sophisticated aspects of writing.

In addition to sequencing tasks, individuals can execute multiple tasks simultaneously by automating fundamental skills. Thus, writers must have handwriting automated if they are going to be able to produce high quality written text.

Role of Automaticity in Enabling High-level Performance

Automaticity refers to the ability to execute skills quickly, accurately and effortlessly. Automaticity allows the use of skills in an effortless way because the skills do not require attention. Thus, an automated skill allows individuals to focus all their attention on the most demanding and sophisticated aspects of complex tasks. In the case of writing, if children need to think about their handwriting, then they cannot think about the most complex and important aspects of writing. However, automaticity in handwriting means that writers can focus all their attention on the most important aspects of writing (eg. generation and organisation of ideas). Proficiency in handwriting enables writers to focus on the key aspects of writing that lead to high quality written text.

Automaticity can only be attained through extensive practice. This means that all students require sufficient practice in forming letters and words to develop automaticity in handwriting.

The Role of Orthographic Motor Integration in Handwriting. Handwriting is a far more sophisticated skill than is generally recognised. Frequently, handwriting is seen as simply a motor skill. However, the ability to write letters and words is more than a motor activity. Handwriting requires the integration of the movements involved in forming of letters with an individual's knowledge of the orthography. 'Orthography' refers to the ways in which letters are sequenced to form words. Thus, handwriting requires a very specific and sophisticated kind of knowledge where writers integrate their knowledge of how English letters work in words with the act of physically forming those letters. This is referred to as orthographic-motor integration.

Effective Approaches to Teaching in Handwriting.

Automaticity in handwriting means that students must be able to write letters and words on the page accurately, quickly and effortlessly. Traditional approaches to teaching handwriting have often focussed on careful replication of letter shapes, precise pencil control and neat, disciplined formation of letters. Research shows that these approaches actually have a negative impact on the development of automaticity and consequently impede children's abilities to produce high quality written text.

We have also found that while traditional teaching approaches are ineffective, there are some teaching approaches that are highly efficacious in promoting proficiency in orthographic-motor integration. Research shows that the key to developing automaticity in handwriting lies in providing students with experiences that facilitate their knowledge of letter shapes and encourage fluency and freedom in replication of the letter shapes. Additionally, experiences that promote children's abilities to retrieve letter shapes from memory are highly effective. In contrast, programs that use the traditional approaches that require children to produce letters within the confines of two or four lines on a page and that stress neatness and disciplined control of physical movements are negatively related to achievement.

Teachers who use elaborate verbal descriptions when teaching handwriting have students whose achievement is lower than teachers who provide only a few verbal cues. Providing students with models with directional arrows and then encouraging them to remember the formation of the letter is more effective than providing letter shapes which students must trace or copy in a precise way.

When teaching handwriting to children in Prep, teachers should begin with pre-writing activities that introduce the key elements of handwriting. After working on pre-writing activities teachers should introduce letters using an approach that has a focus on three elements:

- First, children should be taught correct formation of letters.
- Second, the focus should be on proficiency and fluency rather than careful disciplined pencil movements or neat, precise work. Teachers should teach handwriting in a way that encourages smooth, efficient and fluid strokes.
- Third, children should practise retrieving letter shapes from memory. They should have sufficient practice to become automatic.

Addressing Students with Difficulties in Handwriting

In later years, there is a strong relationship between difficulties in handwriting and students who have difficulty in producing written text. If students can read proficiently but cannot produce written text, then difficulty in handwriting is frequently the underlying cause of their problems. It may seem surprising to suggest that the underlying problem experienced by students who cannot produce high quality written text, is handwriting, but the research is unequivocal on this point.

The foundation for ensuring that students do not develop chronic writing problems begins in Prep. After children have been provided with a range of pre-writing activities and have been introduced to writing letters, their handwriting should be regularly assessed. If children score significantly below age expectations, they should be provided with a program to address their handwriting difficulties. Teachers should provide students with extensive practice in writing each letter. They should be given many activities involving large and fluid movements.

Research shows that providing students with general fine motor activities which are unrelated to handwriting does not impact on proficiency in handwriting and consequently will not lead to improvements in written language. In order to address handwriting problems, students need a carefully structured sequence of activities that helps them to remember the how to produce the shape of each letter. Thus, children should be provided with practice in forming the letter shapes until they attain mastery.

Pencil Grip

There are two ways children can grip a pencil that will promote efficient handwriting. First:

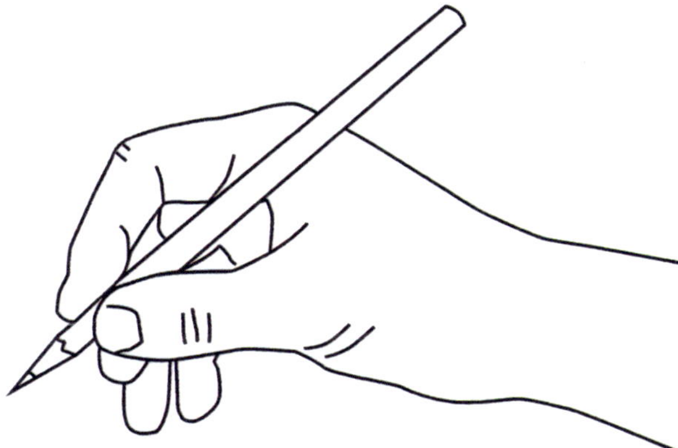

- Children should hold the pencil between the thumb and the first joint of the middle finger.
- The index finger should rest on top of the pencil.
- The pencil should rest on the hand between the thumb and index finger.

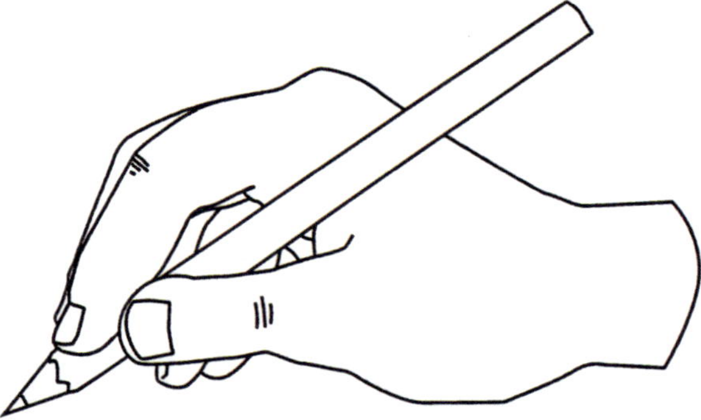

Using the second method, children hold the pencil between the middle finger and thumb rather than resting the pencil on the first joint of the middle finger:

- Children should hold the pencil between the thumb and the middle finger.
- The index finger should rest on top of the pencil.
- The pencil should rest on the hand between the thumb and index finger.

Using other grips can make handwriting more difficult and cumbersome. Children's writing can be slowed by incorrect grips and requires more effort. Consequently, children frequently become fatigued when writing and produce less text of poorer quality.

Posture

- Good posture when writing is essential. Prep is a time when habits will be established that will last the child throughout his or her schooling.
- Children should sit so that their upper body is squarely facing their desks. Their feet should be placed firmly on the floor and their knees at approximately a ninety degree angle.

Their backs should be rested firmly on the back of their chairs, so the weight of their upper body is taken by their buttocks and hamstrings. Their feet should take the weight of their lower legs. Their backs should be straight and shoulders should be back.

Children's chairs should be pulled far enough under their desks so that they can comfortably reach their work without stretching uncomfortably. As far as possible, their elbows should be at about a ninety degree angle and their whole forearm placed on their desks.

Teaching Handwriting to Beginning Writers

There is a developmental sequence that governs children's mastery of handwriting skills. This sequence begins with broad literacy skills.

Phonological Awareness refers to a sensitivity to the sounds people use when they speak. Phonological awareness is a particularly important skill in learning to read. Although it is not directly related to handwriting, it is an essential prerequisite in learning to write.

Before learning to write letters, young children need develop phonological awareness. In particular, they need to learn to rhyme and to identify initial sounds in words.

Letter Knowledge refers to children's understanding of the relationship between the sounds that they can hear in words when they speak and the written letters (or graphemes). Before they learn to write letters, children must learn to recognise the letters. Children should first learn the correspondence between the written letters and the sounds that those letters represent. They can learn letter-names at a later date.

Pre-writing Activities. While children are developing phonological awareness and knowledge of letter-sounds, they should complete the pre-writing activities in LINK Handwriting Prep suitable for students in Prep.

Letter Shapes. After children know the letter-sounds and have had some practice with forming key pencil strokes, they need to learn how to make the shape of each letter. The sequence used to introduce each of the letter shapes should be different from the sequence used to introduce letter-sounds. Some sounds are easier for students to hear than others. For example, the continuants (eg *rrr, mmm, sss*) are easier to hear than the plosives (eg *t, p, d*). Therefore, letter sounds should be introduced in an order so that easy-to-hear letters are introduce before harder to hear letters.

In contrast, the sequence used to introduce written letters should be based on the shape of the letter. Shapes that are easier to make should be introduced before more difficult shapes. The sequence consists of:

- Anti-clockwise circles o, a, c, d
- Vertical lines i, l, t
- Arches m, n, h, r
- Clockwise circles b, p
- Anti-clockwise curves f, e, u
- Hooks g, j, y
- Low frequency and more complex letters qu, w, x, s, k, v, z

Research indicates that effective teachers introduce letters at a fairly rapid rate. Teachers who introduce letter shapes at the rate of one per day have the highest achievement gains.

The focus of teaching handwriting in Prep should be on fluency. Children should be introduced to the letter shapes using large flowing movements. They should be given experiences in activities such as writing letters in the air, writing letters on a desk with their fingers, tracing large sandpaper letters with their fingers, writing letters on a white board, and using finger paint to write letters.

Using Bubble Letters to Write Rainbow Letters with Coloured Pencils

After children have been introduced to each letter shape using a broad range of activities involving large movements, they should begin using pencils to write letters. Rainbow letters are a very effective way of facilitating early handwriting skills. Children are given bubble letter-shapes and produced letters inside the bubbles in a variety of colours.

- First, reinforce correct pencil grip and posture.
- Second, inform children of the correct letter shape. Demonstrate writing the letter on a white board. Give children short verbal cues, not extensive verbal directions (eg. say something like: '*begin, down, around* ..'). Extensive verbal instructions which should not be used would include something like, '*move in the direction of the arrow, go down in a straight line, then make sure you make a curve*...')

Guide children's practice of the letter shape using large fluid movements (eg writing in the air, finger painting, writing in sand, tracing sandpaper letters, writing on desks). This practice should be extensive.

Children complete rainbow letters inside bubble letter shapes in their workbooks. Ask children to select four different coloured pencils. They should open the page at the letter they are working on and write the letter inside the letter shape. Tell them to begin at the green dot, follow the directional arrow and end at the red dot.

References and Further Reading

Berninger, V. (1999),Coordinating transcription and text generation in working memory during composing: Automatic and constructive processes. Learning Disabilities Quarterly, 22,: 99-112

Berninger, V., Abbott, R., Rogan, L., Reed, E., Abbott, S., Brooks, A., Vaughan, K. and Graham, S. (1998), Teaching spelling to children with specific learning disabilities: The mind's eye ear and eye brat the computer or pencil. Learning Disabilities Quarterly, 21, 106-122.

Berninger, V., Rutberg, J., Abbott, R., Garcia, N., Anderson-Youngstrom, A., Brooks and Fulton C. (2006). Tier 1 and tier 2 early intervention for handwriting and composing, Journal of School Psychology. 44, 3-30.

Berninger, V., Vaughn, K., Abbott, R., Abbott, S., Rogan, L., Brooks, A., Reed, E., and Graham, S. (1997). Treatment of handwriting problems in beginning writers: Transfer from handwriting to composition. Journal of Educational Psychology, 89: 652-666.

Berninger, V., Yates, C., Cartwright, A., Rutberg, J., Remy E., and Abbott, R. (1992). Lower-level developmental skills in beginning writing. Reading and Writing: An Interdisciplinary Journal, 4, 257-280

Christensen, C. (2004), Relationship between orthographic-motor integration and computer use for the production of creative and well-structured written text. British Journal of Educational Psychology, 74, 551-564.

Christensen, C. (2005). The role of orthographic-motor integration in the production of creative and well-structured written text for students in secondary school. Educational Psychology 25; 441-453

Christensen. C., and Jones, D. (2000). Handwriting: An underestimated skill in the development of written language. Handwriting Today, 2, 56-69.

Graham, S. (1990). The role of production factors in learning disabled students' compositions. Journal of Educational Psychology, 82, 781-791.

Graham, S., Harris, K. and Fink, B. (2000). Is handwriting causally related to learning to write? Treatment of handwriting problems in beginning writers. Journal of Educational Psychology, 92, 620-633.

Graham, S., and Weintraub, N. (1996). A review of handwriting research: Progress and prospects from 1980 to 1994. Educational Psychology Review, 8, 7-87.

Graham, S., Weintraub, N., and Berninger, V. (1998). The relationship between handwriting style and speed and legibility. Journal of Educational Research, 91, 290-296.

Jones, D. and Christensen, C. (1999) 'Relationship between automaticity in handwriting and students' ability to generate written text', Journal of Educational Psychology, 91(1): 44-49.

Medwell, J., and Wray, D. (2007). Handwriting: What do we know and what do we need to know?. Literacy, 41, 10-15.

Schlagal, B. (2007). Best practices in spelling and handwriting. S. Graham, C. MacArthur, J. Fitzgerald (eds.) Best Practices in Writing Instruction: Solving Problems in the Teaching of Literacy. Guliford Press: NY, (pp 179-201)

Smits-Engelsman, B. and Van Galen, G. (1997). Dysgraphia in children: Lasting deficiency or transient developmental delay?. Journal of Experimental Child Psychology. 67, 164-184.

Sudsawad, P., Trombly, C., Henderson, A. and Tickle-Degnen, L. (2002). Testing the effect of kinesthetic training on handwriting performance in first-grade students. American Journal of Occupational Therapy, 56, 26-33.

Yates, C., Berninger, V. and Abbott, R. (1994). Writing problems in intellectually gifted children. Journal for the Education of the Gifted, 18, 131-155.

Assessing Handwriting

Teachers should ensure that all students have attained fluency in writing letters by using regular monitoring assessments. For children in Year 1 this monitoring assessment consists of asking children to write the alphabet in order. They should write all lower case letters first. Then if they have sufficient time they can then write the capitals. Children will only be given a minute to do this.

To implement the assessment:

1. Teachers should distribute copies of the sentence to all children. Children should also have a pencil.

2. Children's names should be located at the top of the assessment.

3. Tell Children that they are going to write the letters of the alphabet in order. Tell children that they have only one minute to do this. They should not begin until they are told they can pick up their pencils and they should stop immediately the time is up. Tell children that they should begin with "little letters", if they have finished all the "little letters" and still have time, they can write the capitals.

4. Set a timer for 1 minute. When everyone is ready, start the timer and tell children to begin copying the sentence

5. After one minute has elapsed, tell all children to stop work. It is essential that children stop copying the sentence immediately after one minute.

Scoring the Assessment

To score the assessment, count the number of letters that students have written in correct order. To do this look at each pair of letters, if children have written 'a' as the first letter, they score one point. Then for every letter that follows in correct order, score one additional point. Thus, if they write 'b' after the 'a', they score another point (total 2 points). But if they have written 'c' after 'a' they do not get another point (total only 1 point).

Judge children's scores on this measure at the end of Prep/beginning Year 1 and end of Year 1 based on the following table:

	End of Prep	End of Yr 1
Excellent	28	30
Good	20	26
Average	17	20
Below Average	12	15
Seriously Below Average	6	8
Goal	22	24

Thus, children who score more than 28 at the beginning of the year and more than 30 at the end of the year are performing exceptionally well. Many children will score 17 at the beginning of the year and 20 at the end of the year. This is an average score but is not sufficient to ensure proficiency. The aim of the handwriting program should be to have every child score at least 24 on the assessment at the end of Year 1. Teachers should use the assessment to tr y to ensure that all children reach this score by the end of the Year 1.

Children who score below 12 at the beginning of the year are at risk of developing difficulties in handwriting. This has the potential to impact on the ability to produce written text. They should be carefully monitored and given more experience with writing large, free-flowing letters.

Children who score below 6 have serious difficulties in learning to write letters. They need to be provided with a specifically designed program and to repeat activities with bubble letters until they become proficient.

Handwriting LINK Assessment Year 1

Name __________________________Class ____________________

Write the letters of the alphabet in order. Begin with small letters then write the capitals. If you finish all the alphabet then write the letters again. You will only have one minute. You should write as many letters as you can for one minute. Do not begin until your teacher tells you and put your pencil down as soon as the minute is up but remember to keep writing for the full minute.

Directions for Implementing the Program.

Writing Bubble Letters

1. **Use a developmental sequence**

Teachers should ensure that children are at an appropriate developmental level before introducing handwriting. Begin with phonological awareness. Phonological awareness refers to the ability to hear the sounds in spoken language. In particular, children should be able to hear rhymes and initial sounds in words. Children also need to know letter-sounds correspondences. If children cannot rhyme, identify initial sounds and identify the sounds that letters represent, then they are not ready to begin handwriting. Time should be taken to teach these skills and when they are mastered, writing letters can begin.

2. **Teacher demonstration to introduce letters one at a time.**

The first step in each lesson in this workbook is teacher demonstration. When teaching how to write letters, teachers should focus on developing fluency and proficiency as well as promoting children's ability to recall letter-shapes from memory. First demonstrate how to write each letter by making the letter in the air and writing it on a white board.

3. **Provide extended practice in making letter shapes** using large fluid movements. Give children time to practise making the letter using a variety of activities. These would include:

- Writing letters in the air
- Writing on a flat surface (eg desks)
- Finger painting letters
- Tracing letters on sandpaper shapes
- Writing letters in sand

4. **Introduce writing each letter in workbooks using rainbow letters in bubble shapes.**

- Children select four coloured pencils
- Children write rainbow letters within the bubble shape. They should begin at the green dot, follow the directional arrow and stop at the red dot.
- When guiding students' strokes, teachers should provide short verbal cues.

Writing Letters on a Single Line

1. **Teachers' Demonstration**. When children have been introduced to all letters using bubble letters they can complete activities with letters on a single line. The focus should continue to be on teaching children fluency in production of letters and for children to recall the shapes from memory. The single line should be seen as a guide for placement of the letter, not as a mechanism to restrict fluency in creating the shape. Teachers should demonstrate how to write the letter on a single line by writing it repeatedly on a whiteboard.

2. **Children Practise Letter Shapes** using large fluid movements. Give children practice in making the letter using a variety of activities. These would include:

- Writing letters in the air
- Writing on a flat surface (eg desks)
- Writing letters on a whiteboard.

3. **Children complete page in Workbook**. Children should write letter shapes in the bubble letter and then complete each line in the workbook.

Writing Letters on a Double Lines

When children have completed all the single-line pages in the workbook, they will be ready to begin writing within double lines. At this stage, children should have mastery of making the shape and are ready to focus on fitting the letter using the constraints of the lines. The same steps should be followed as in completing other activities in the workbook:

1. **Teacher's demonstration.**
2. **Children practise letter shapes**
3. **Children complete page in workbook**

Bubble Letters

Blank page intentionally added.

octopus

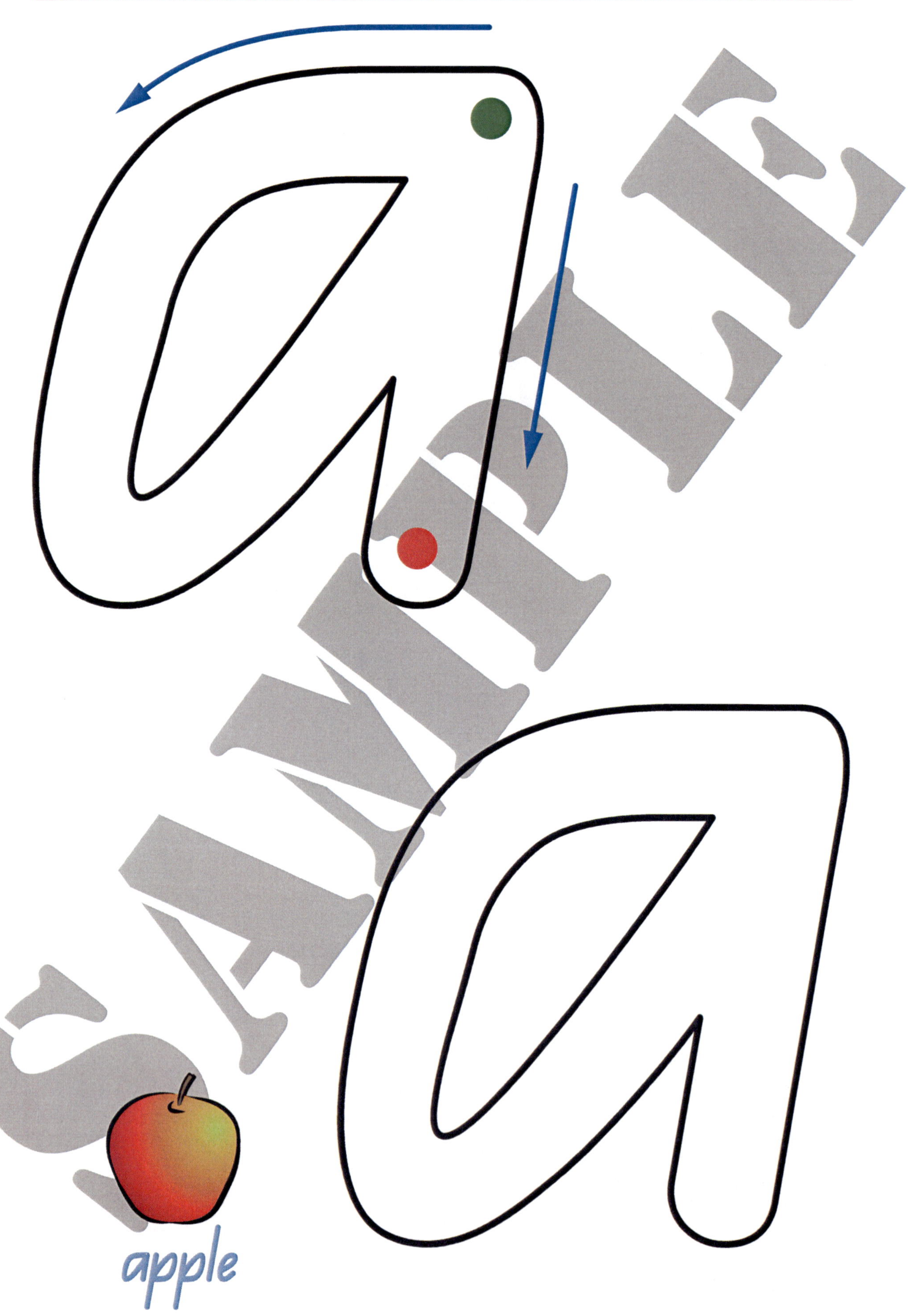
apple

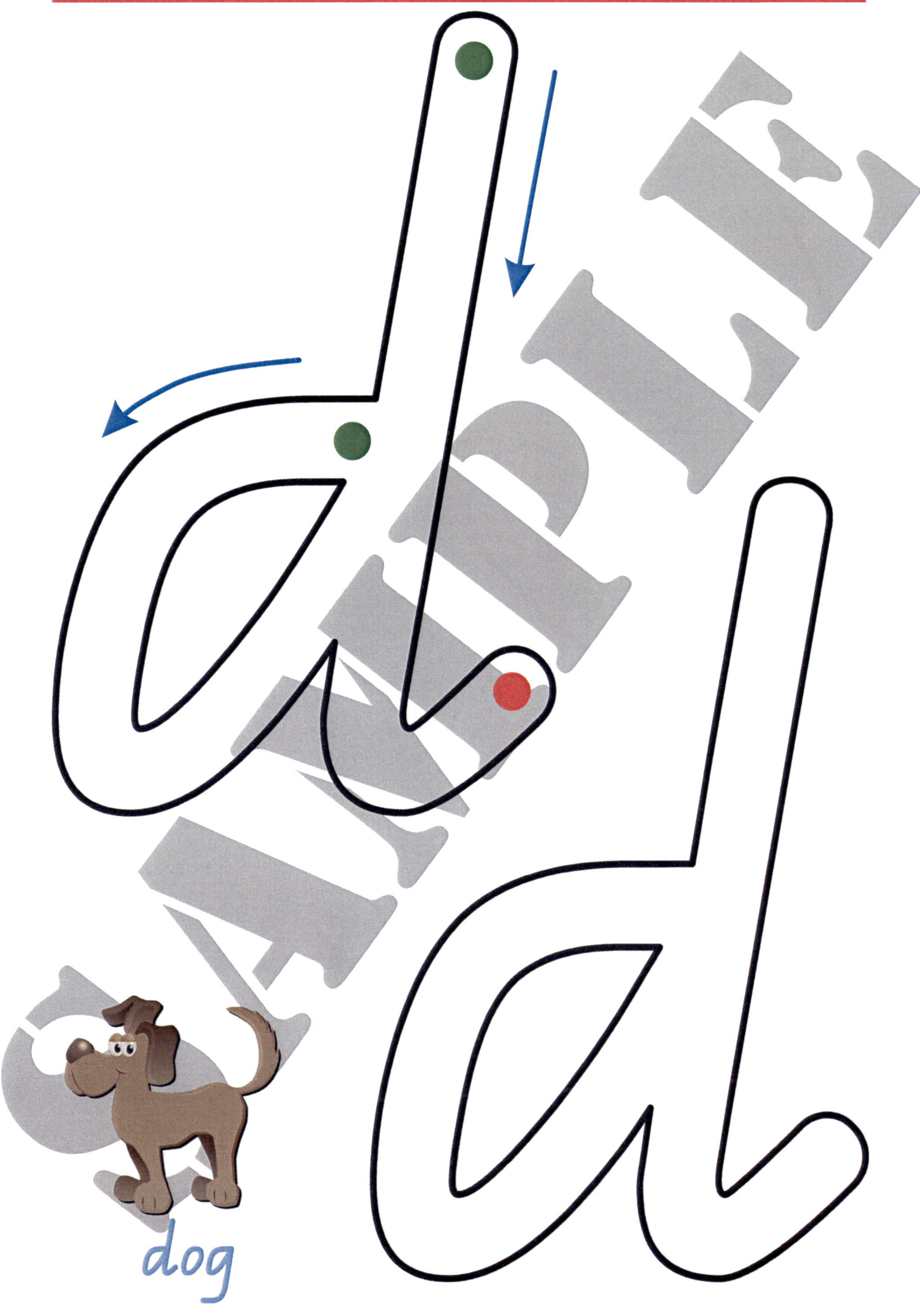
dog

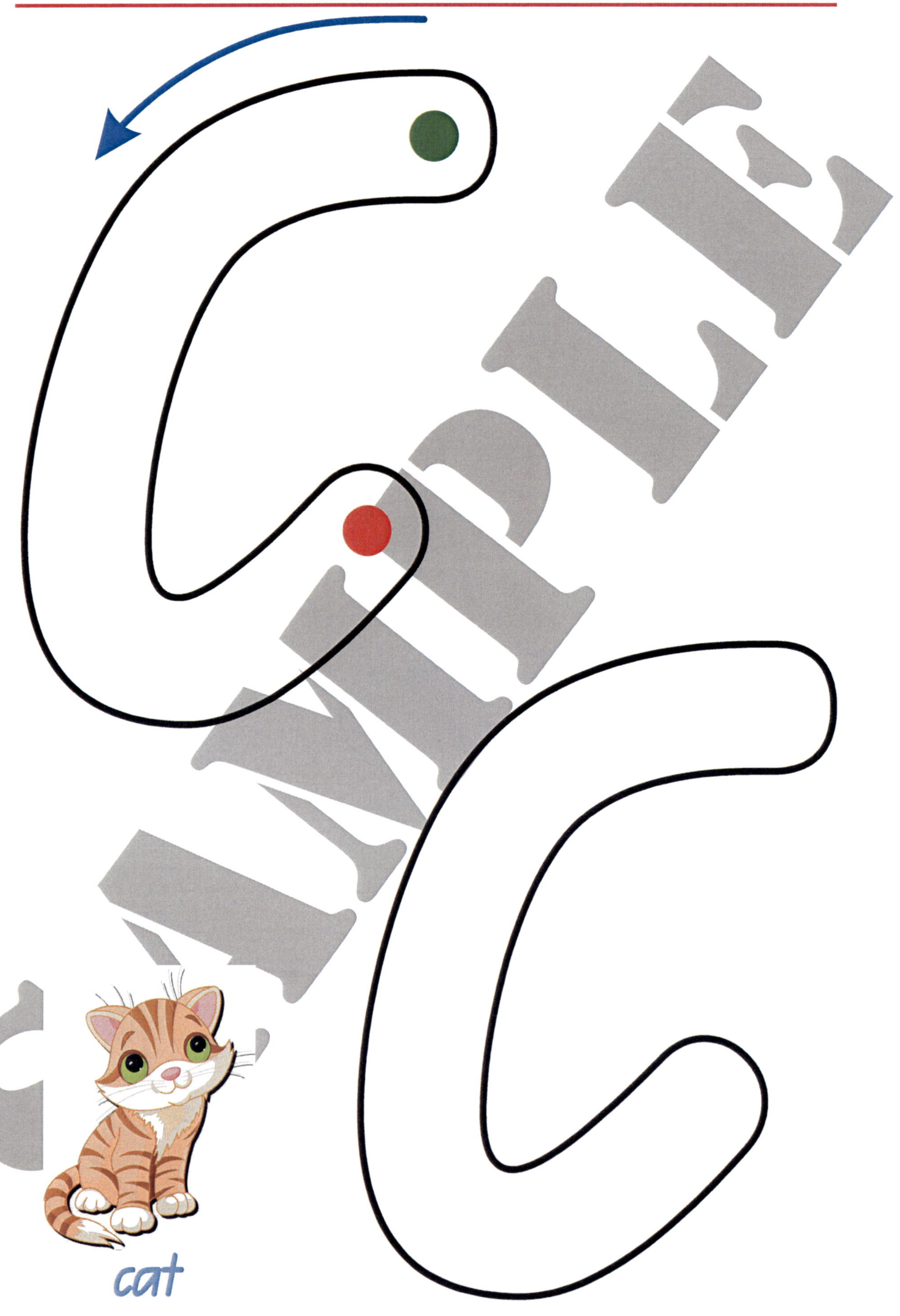
SAMPLE
cat

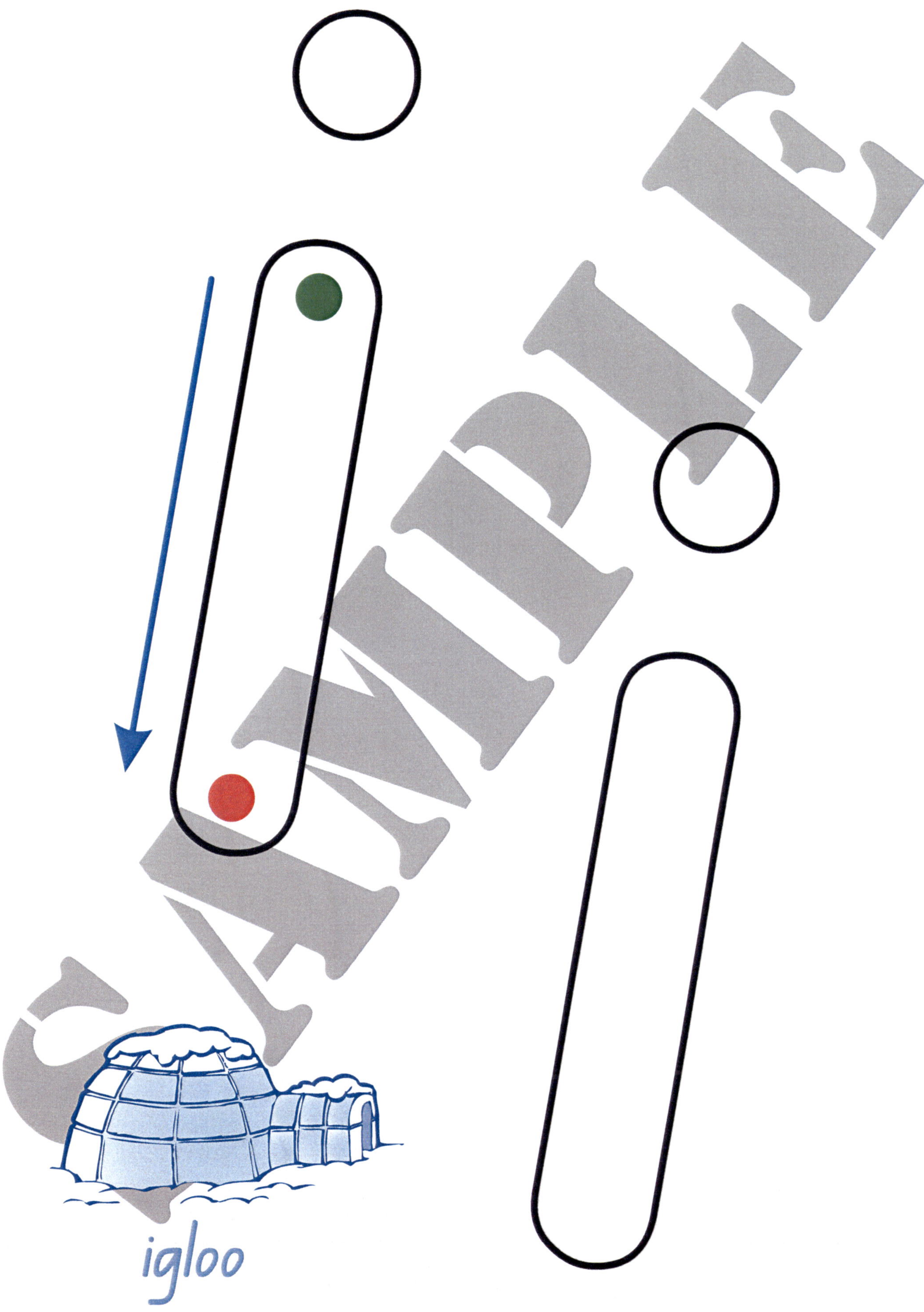
igloo

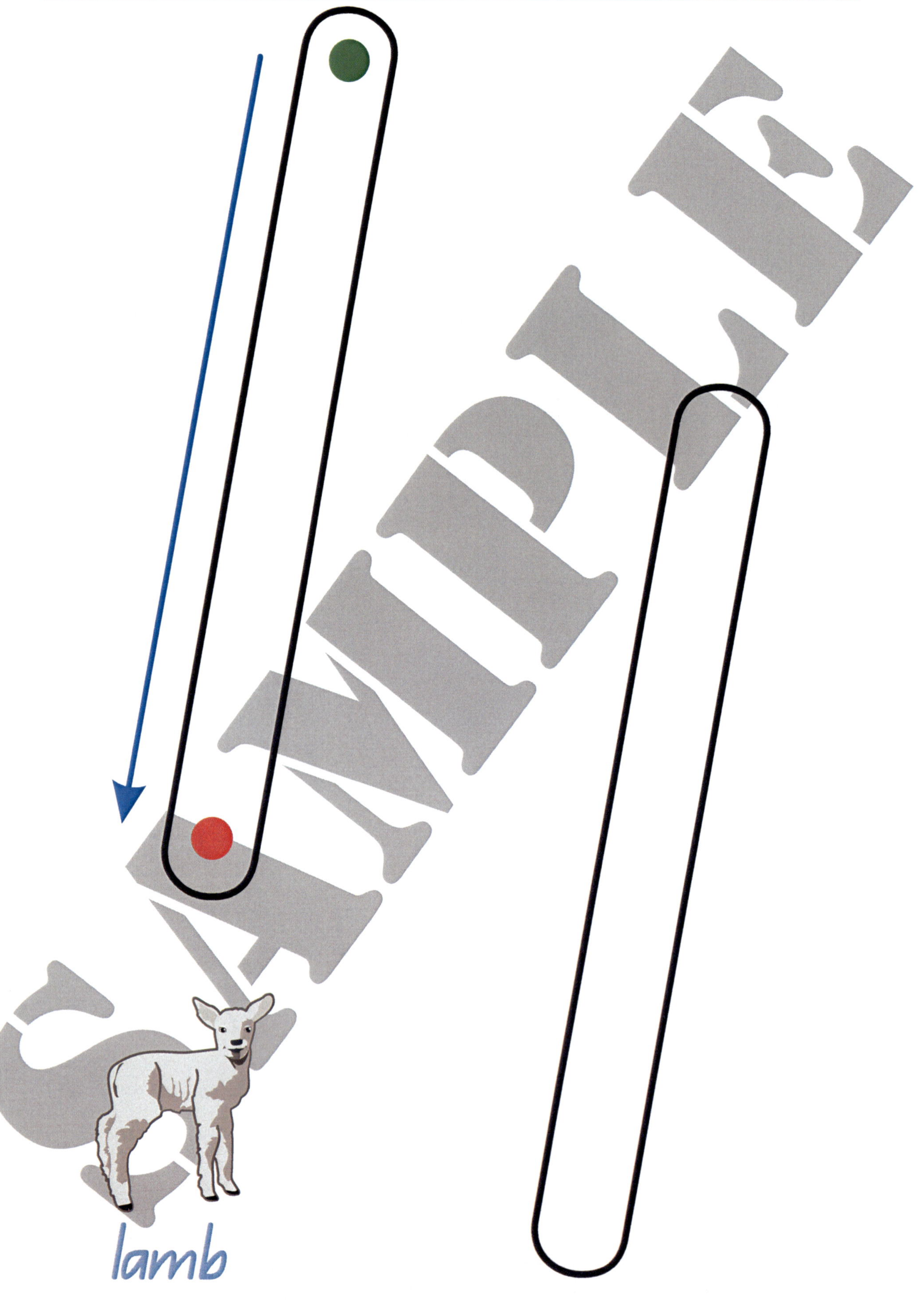
lamb

tiger

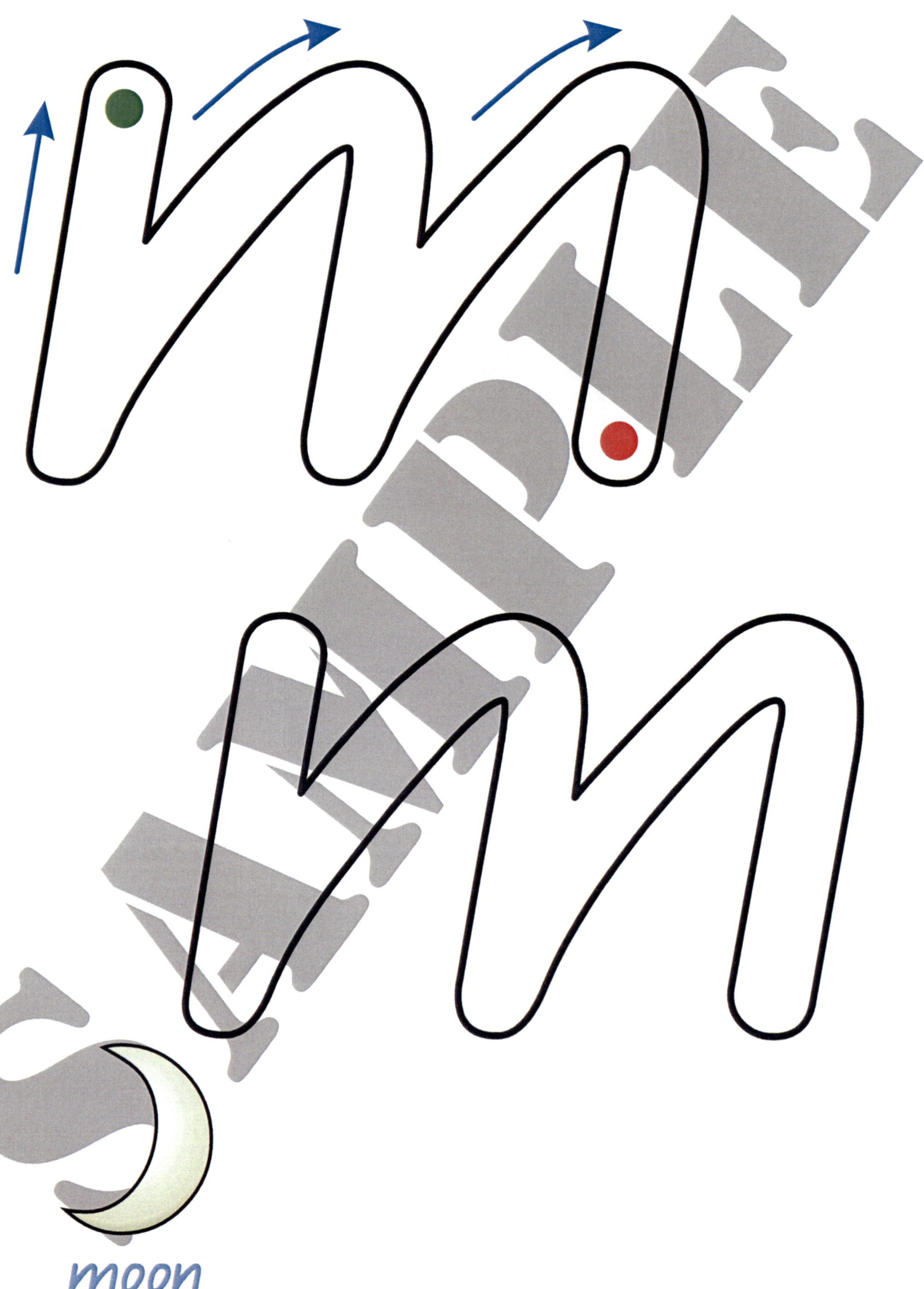
moon

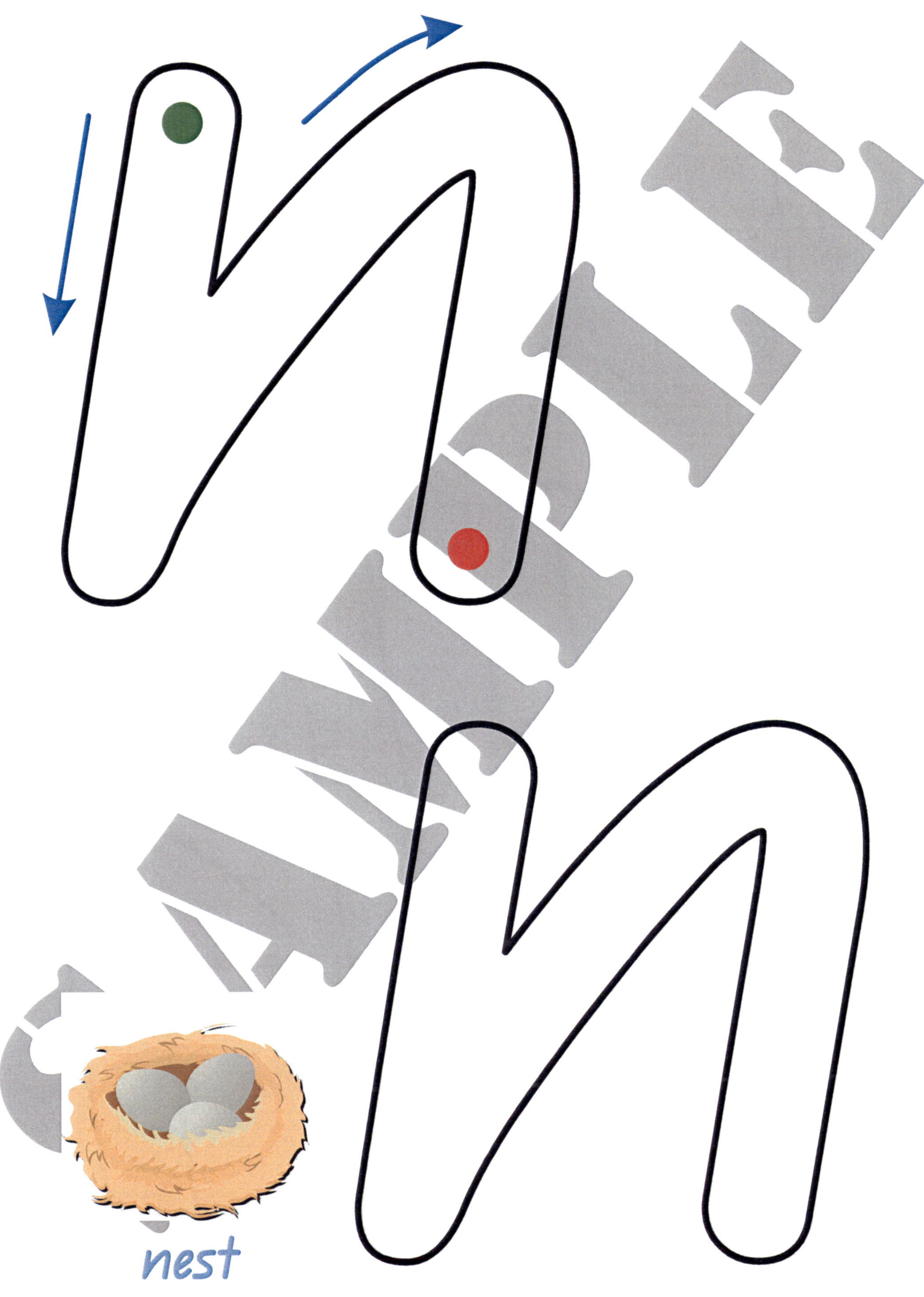
nest

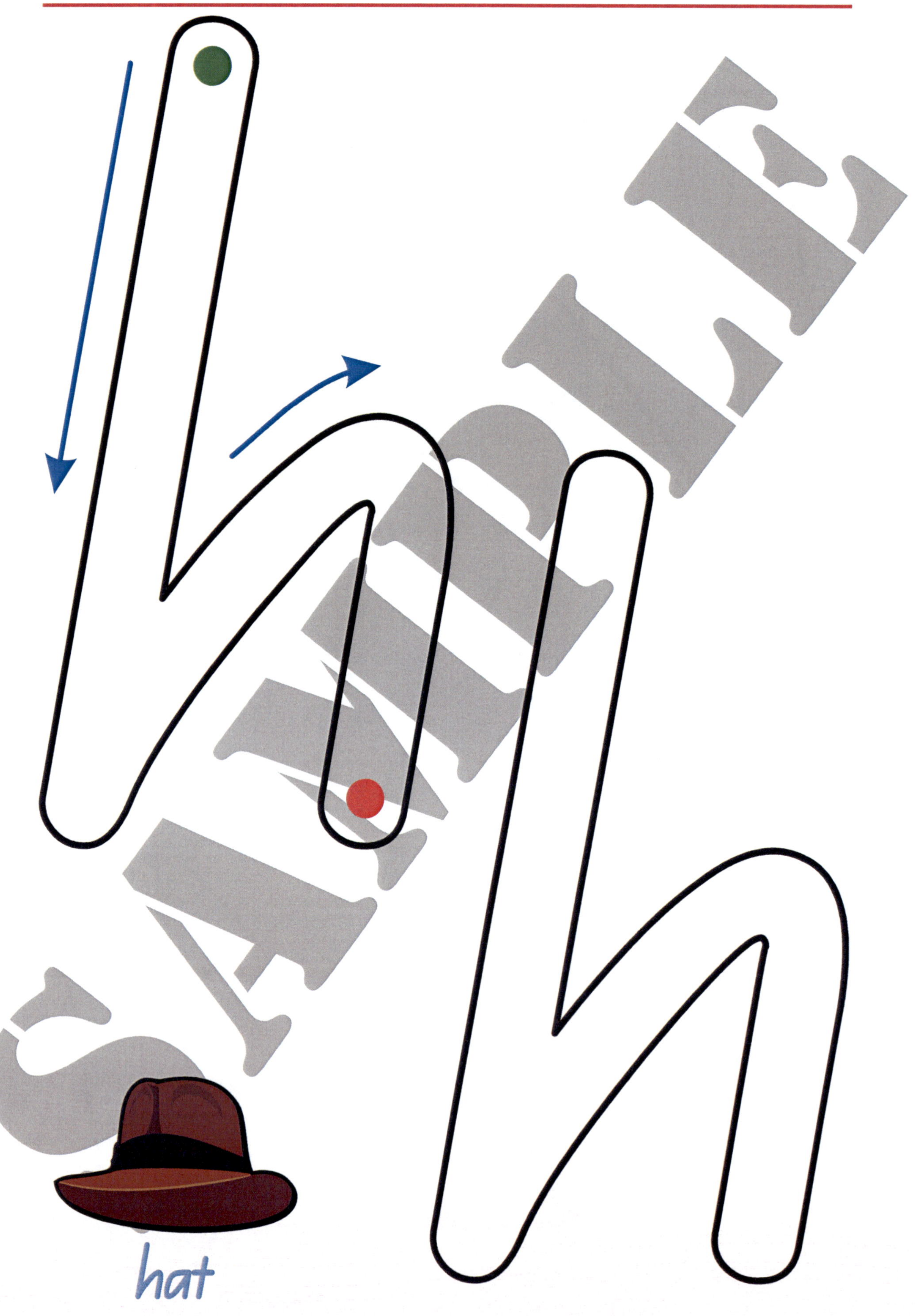
hat

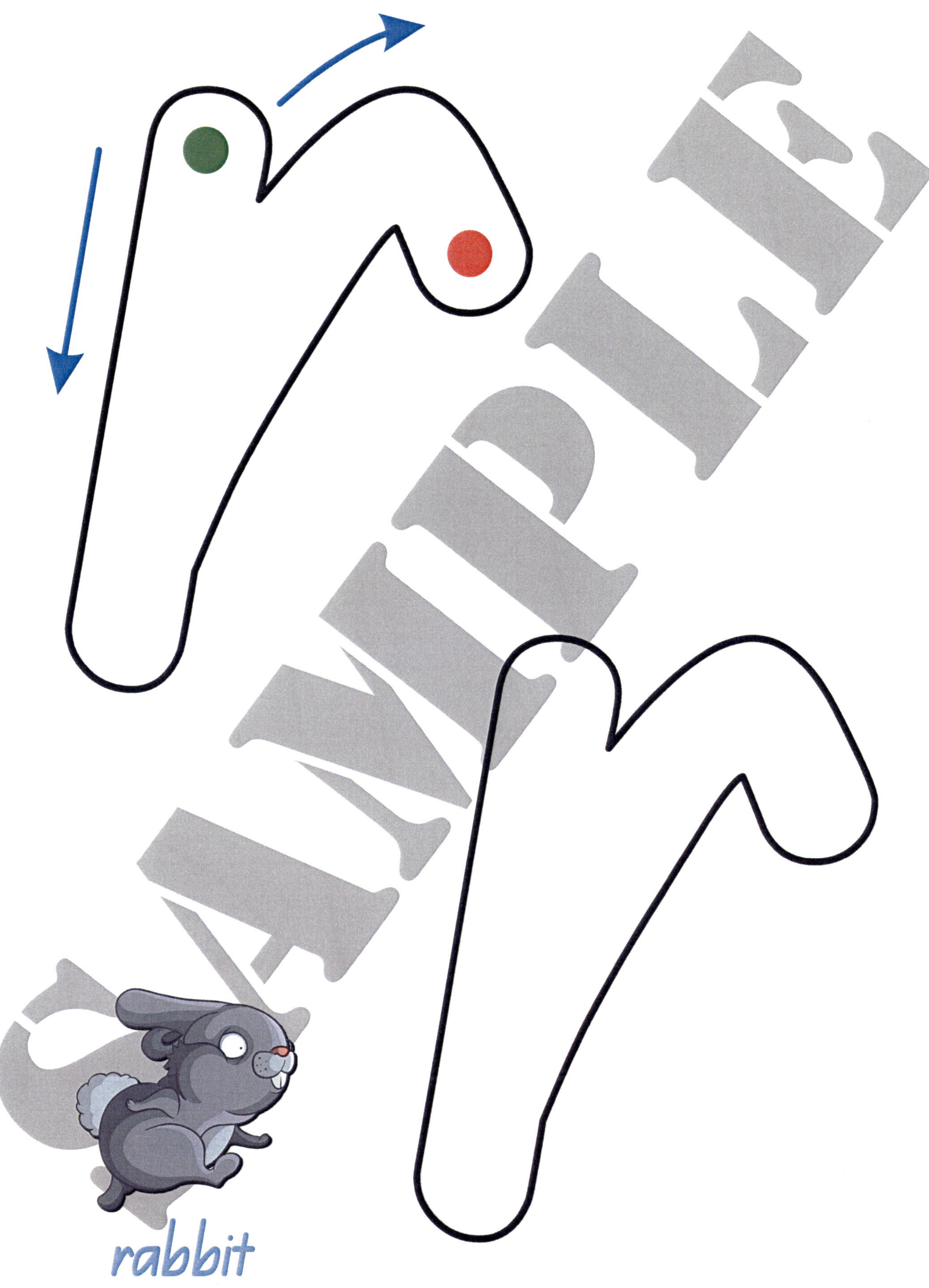
SAMPLE
rabbit

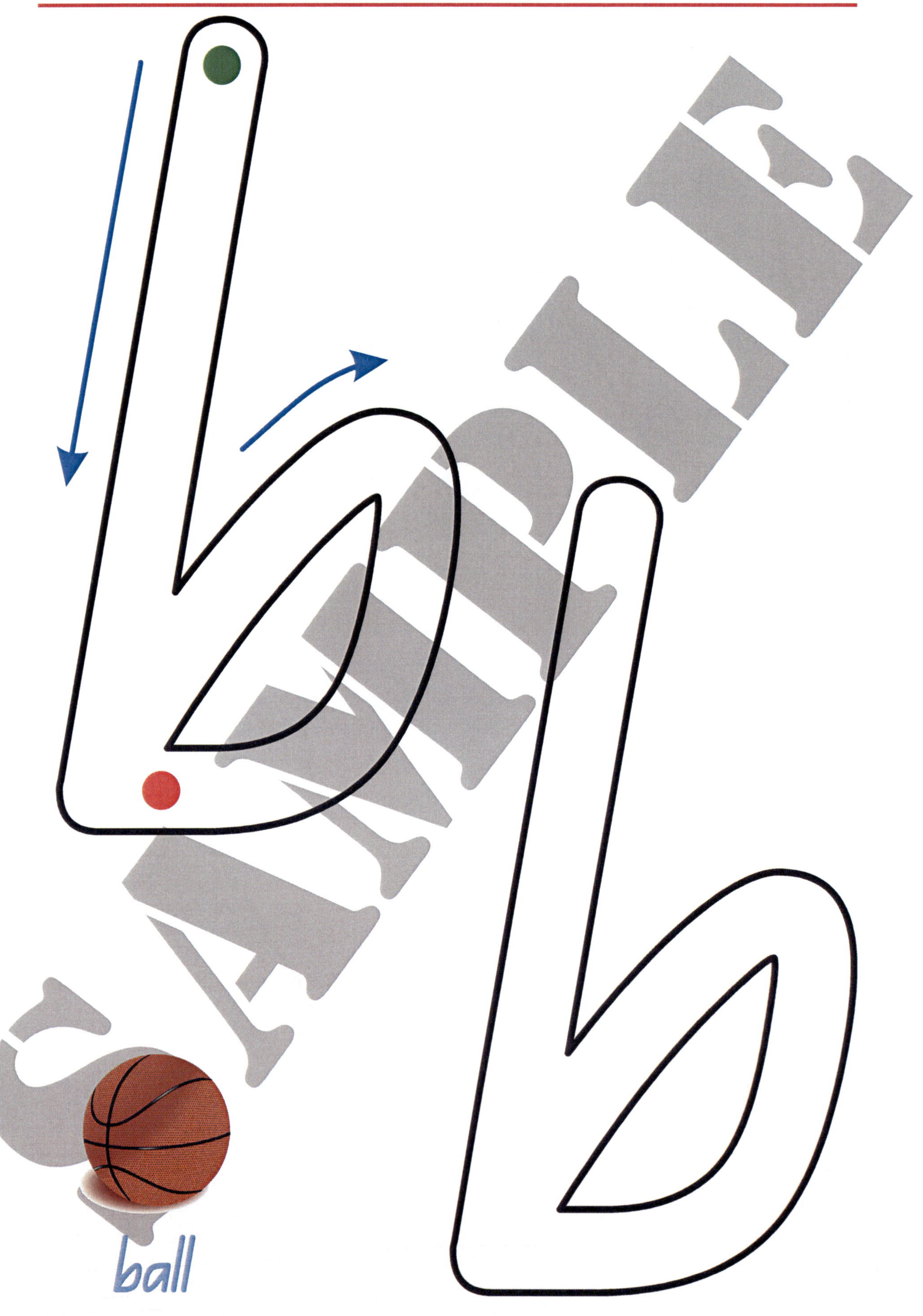
ball

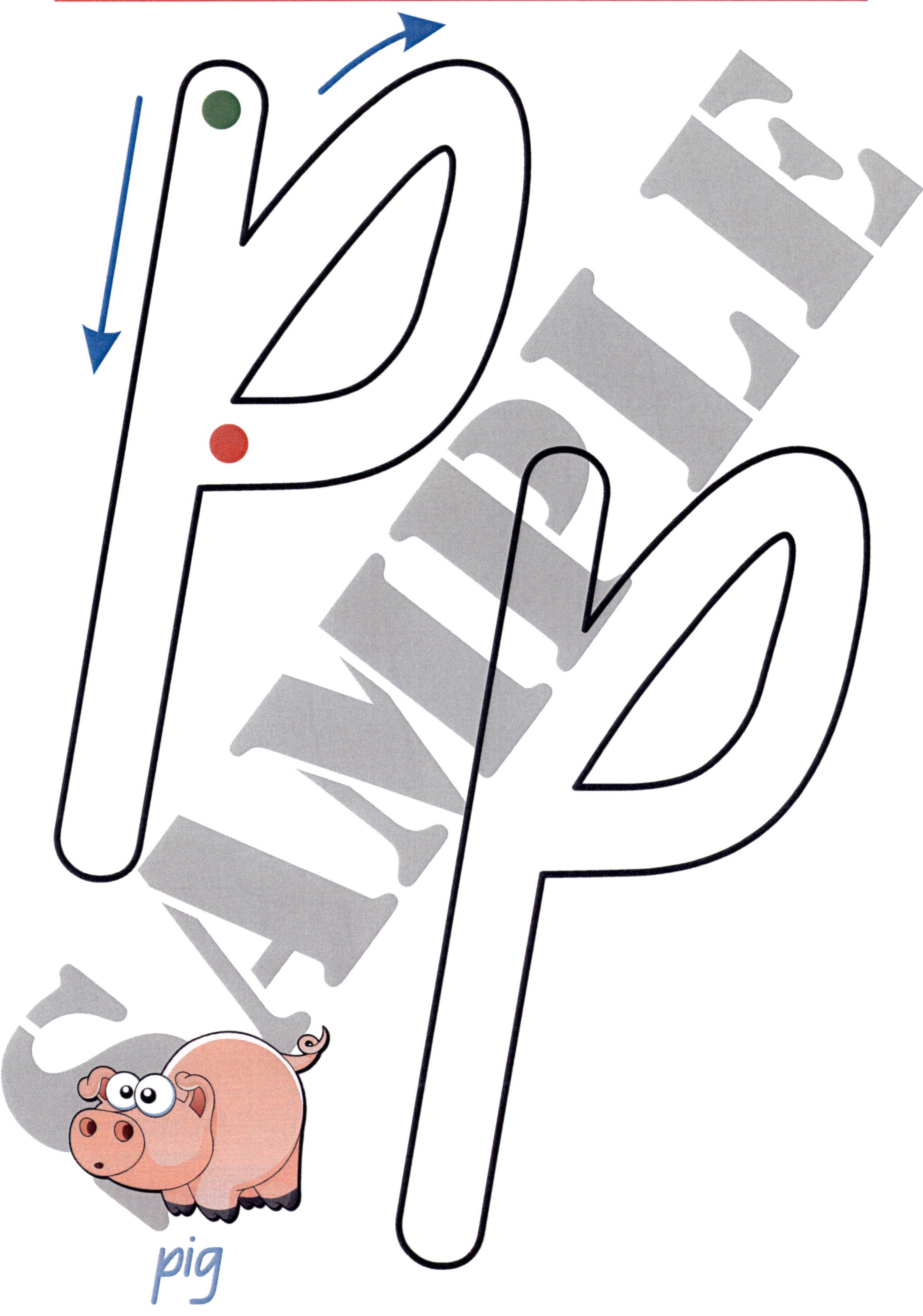
SAMPLE
pig

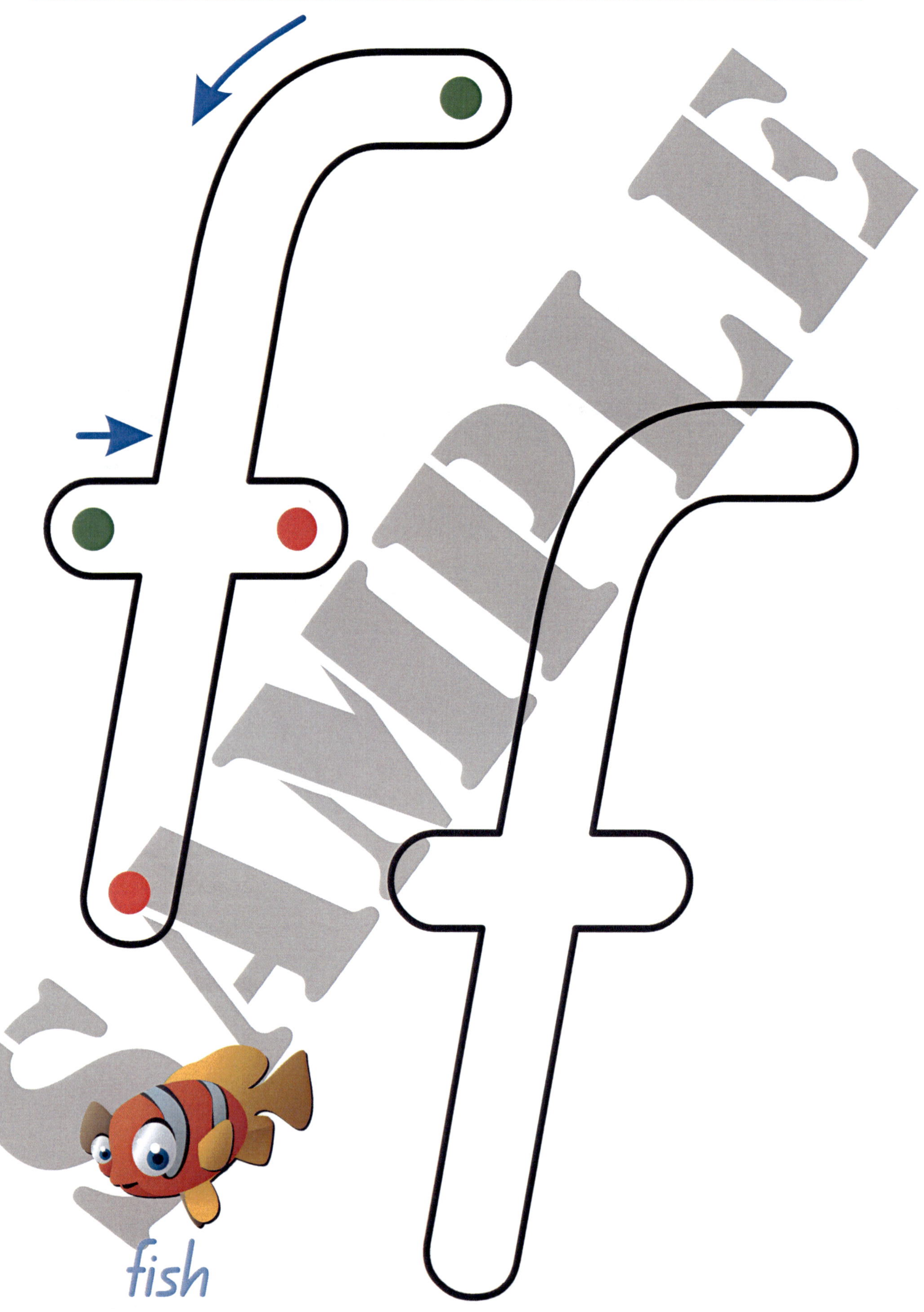
fish

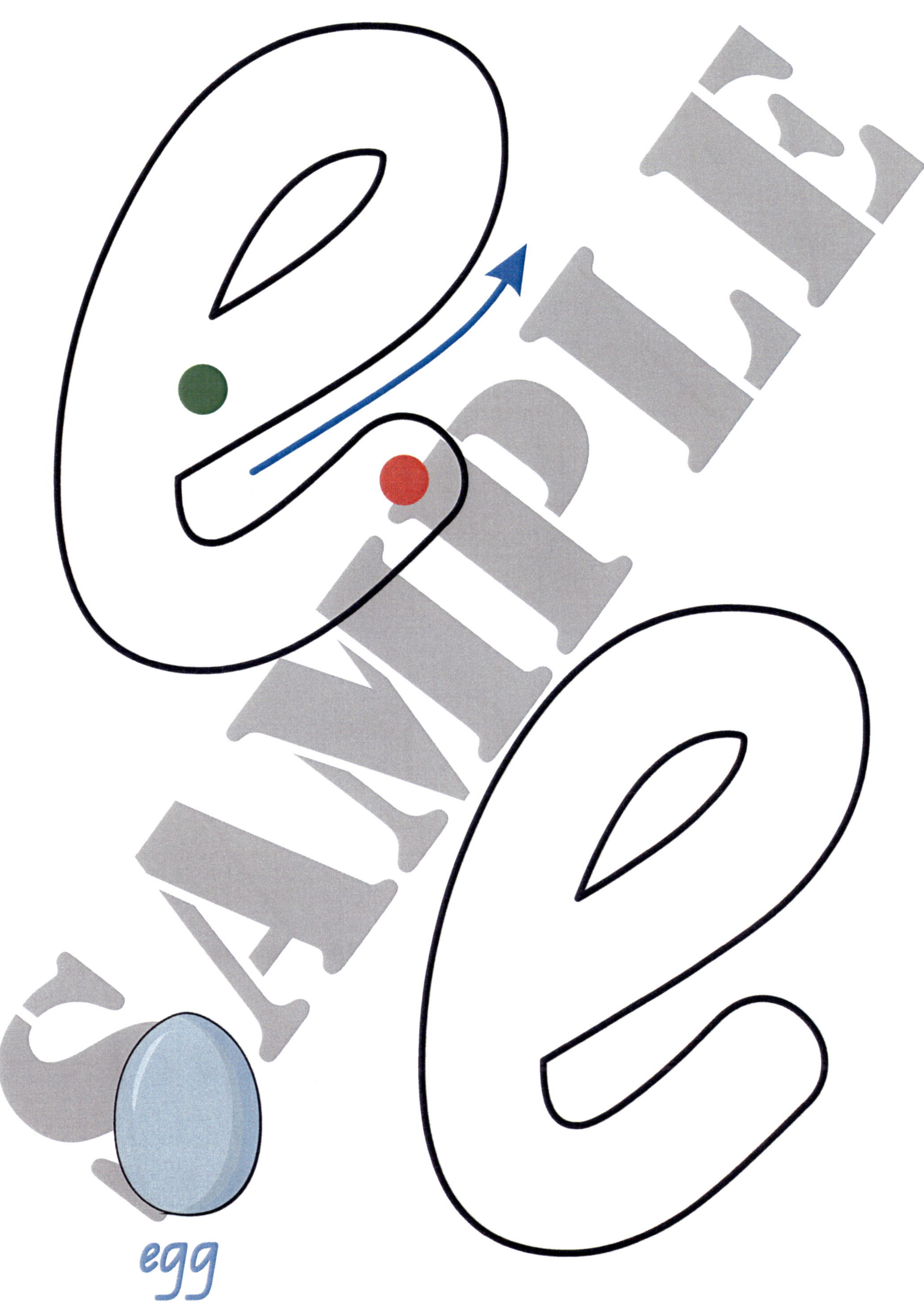
egg

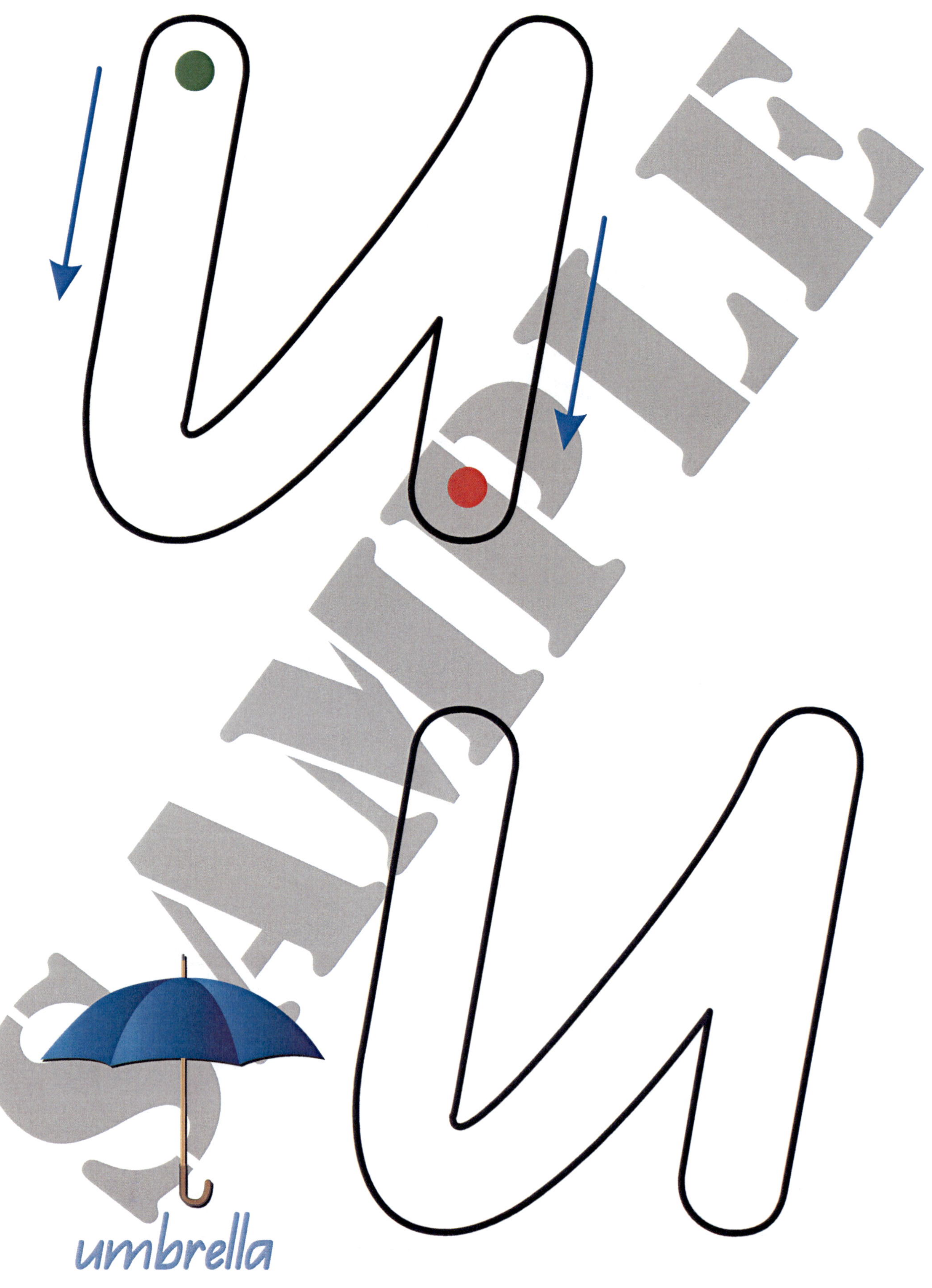

umbrella

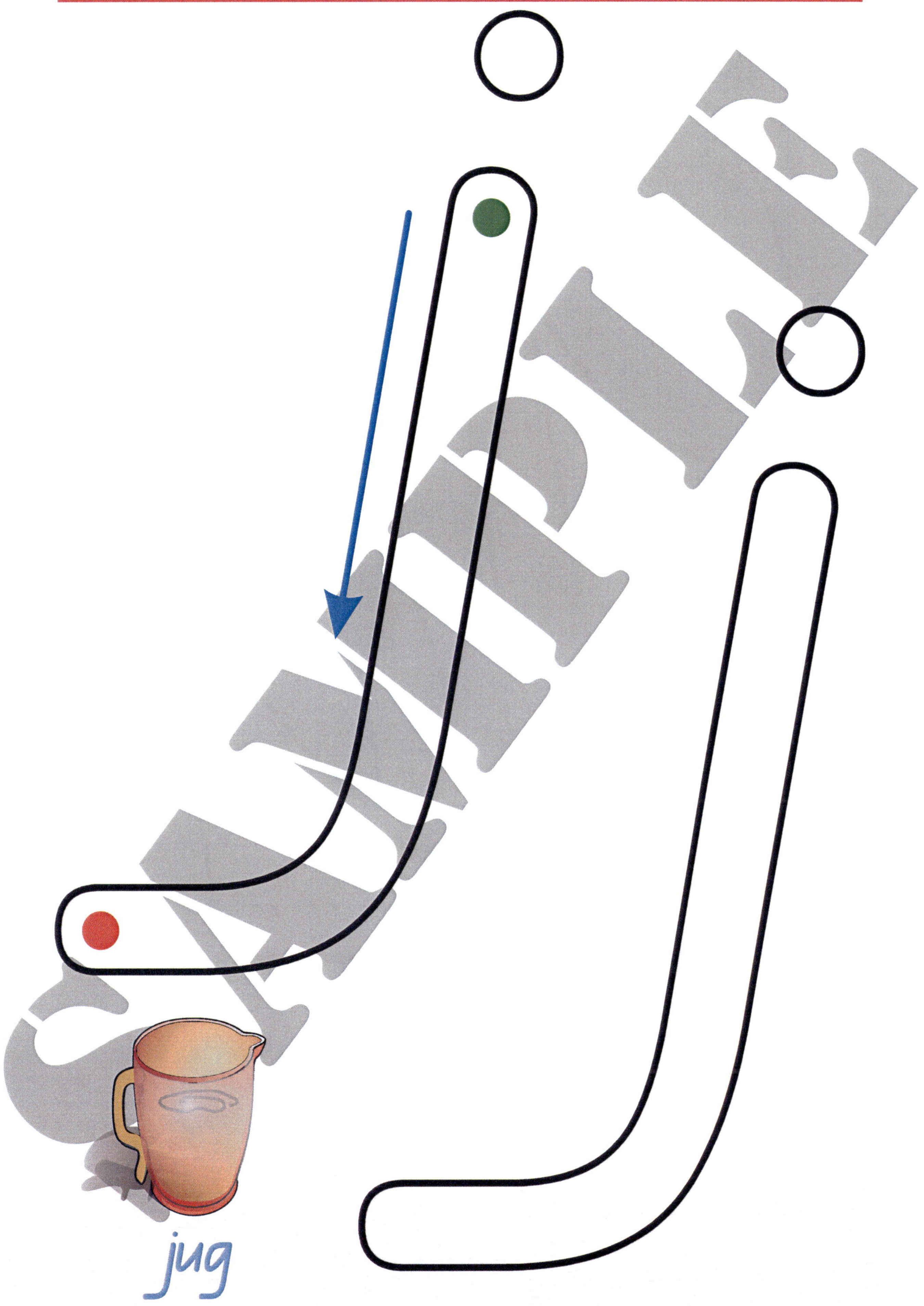
jug

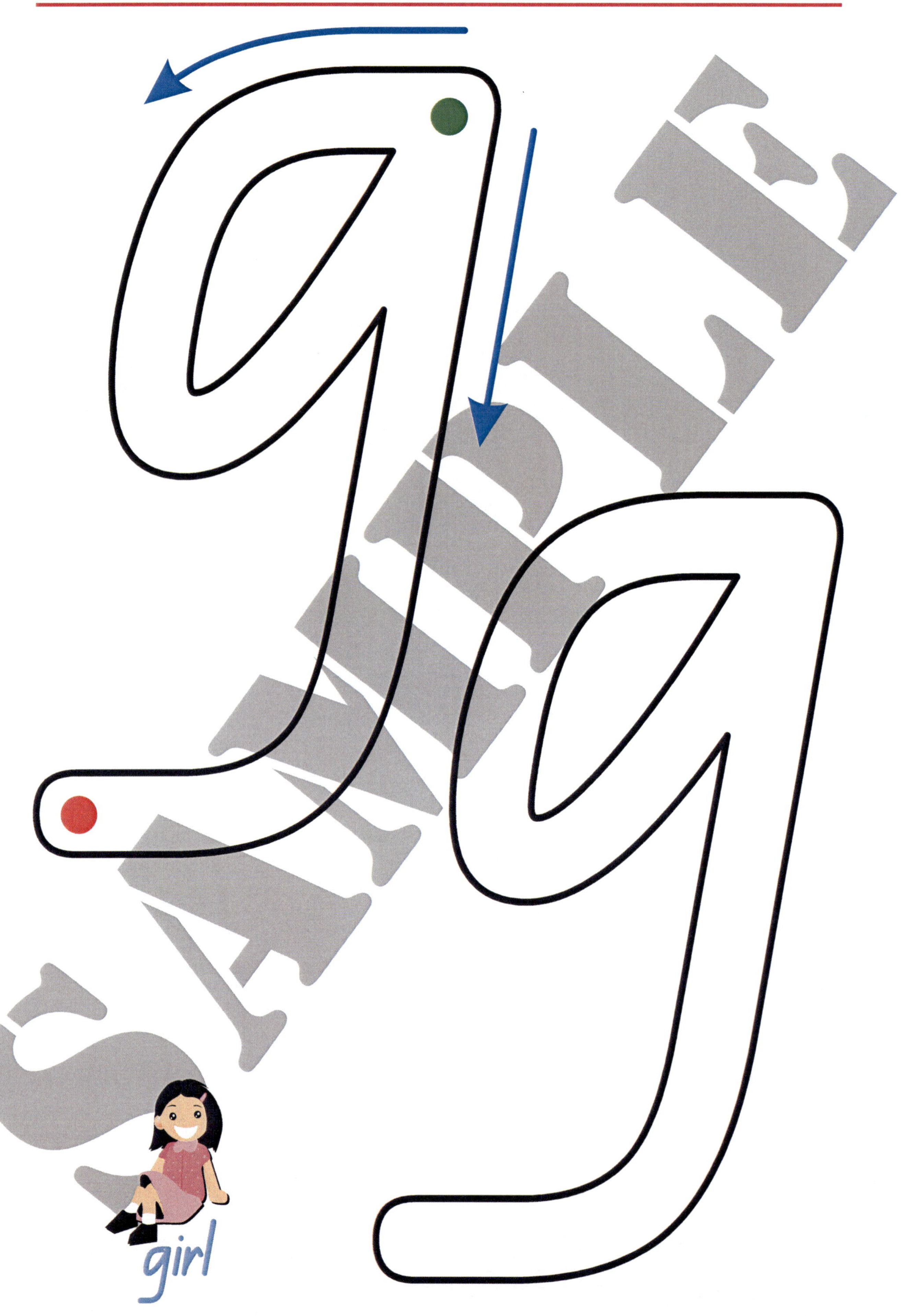
girl

queen

witch

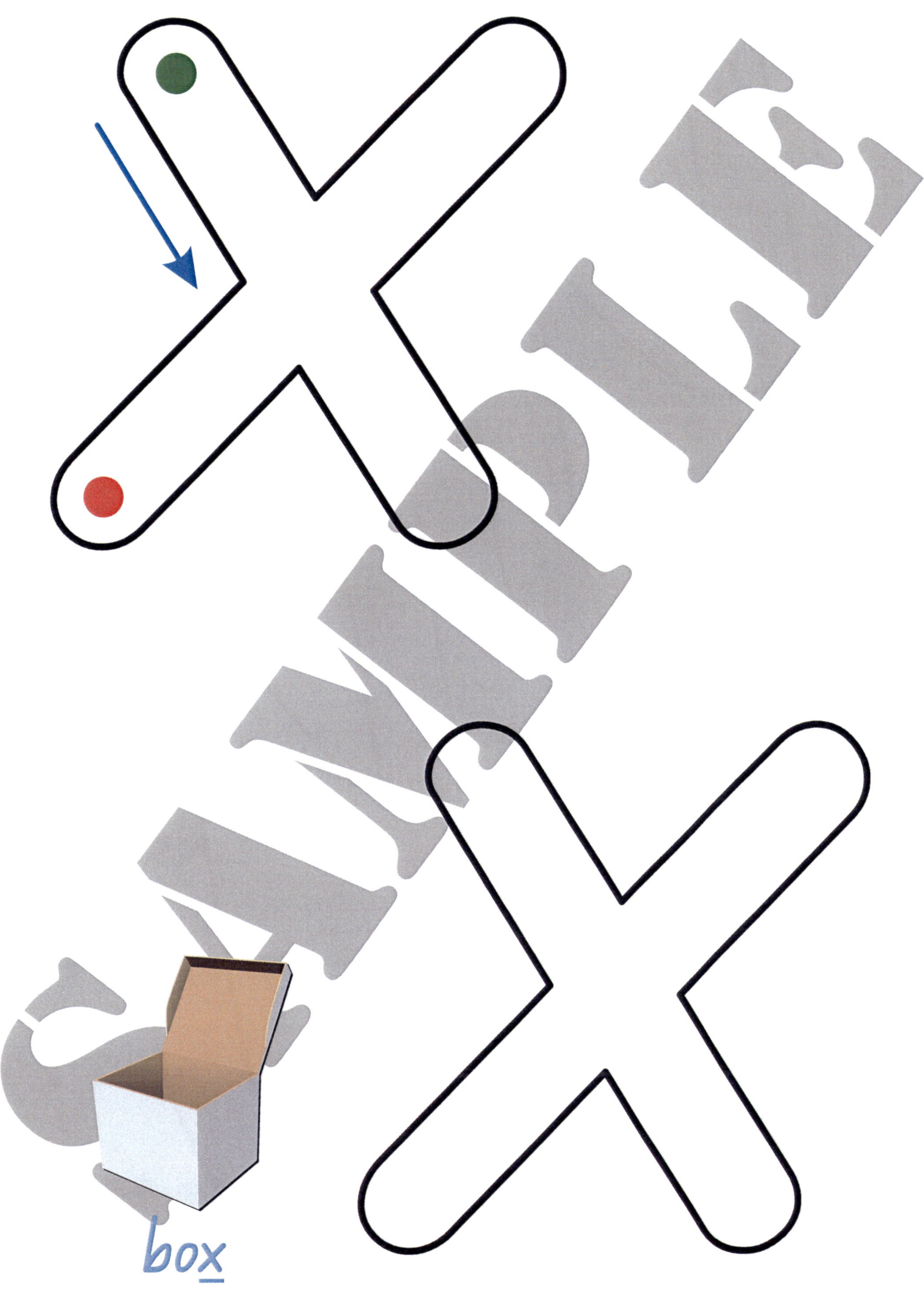
SAMPLE
box

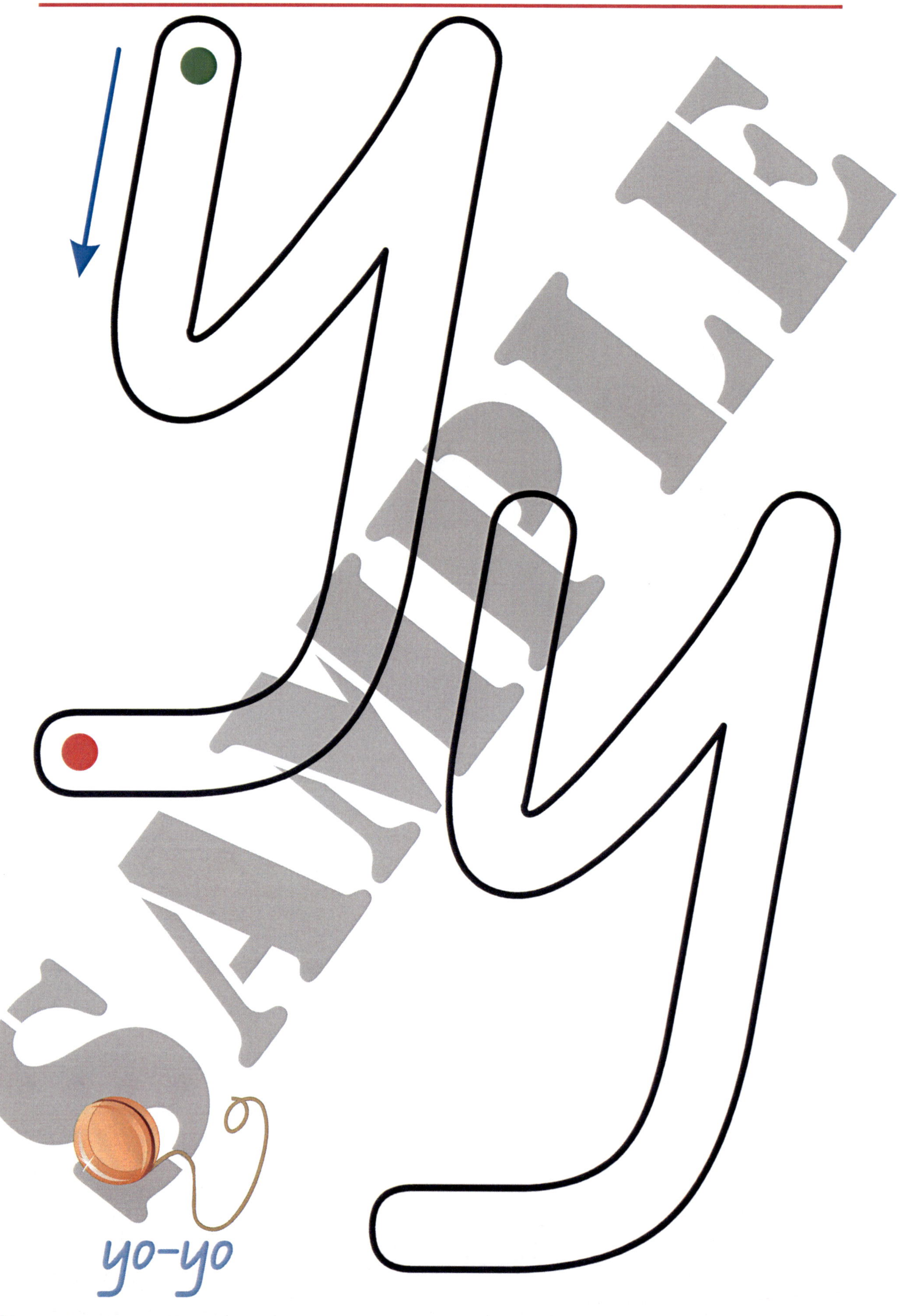
yo-yo

SAMPLE
sun

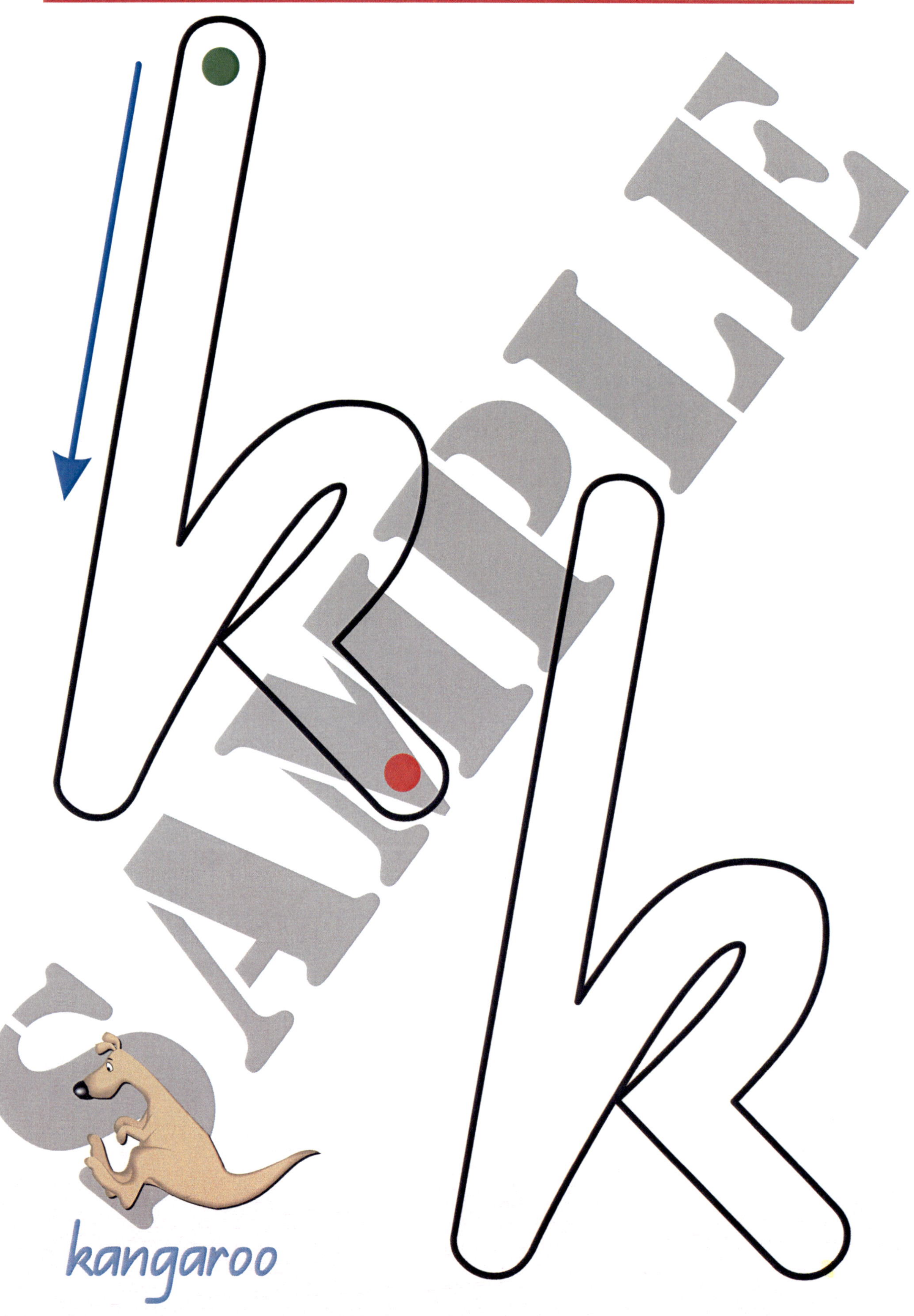
kangaroo

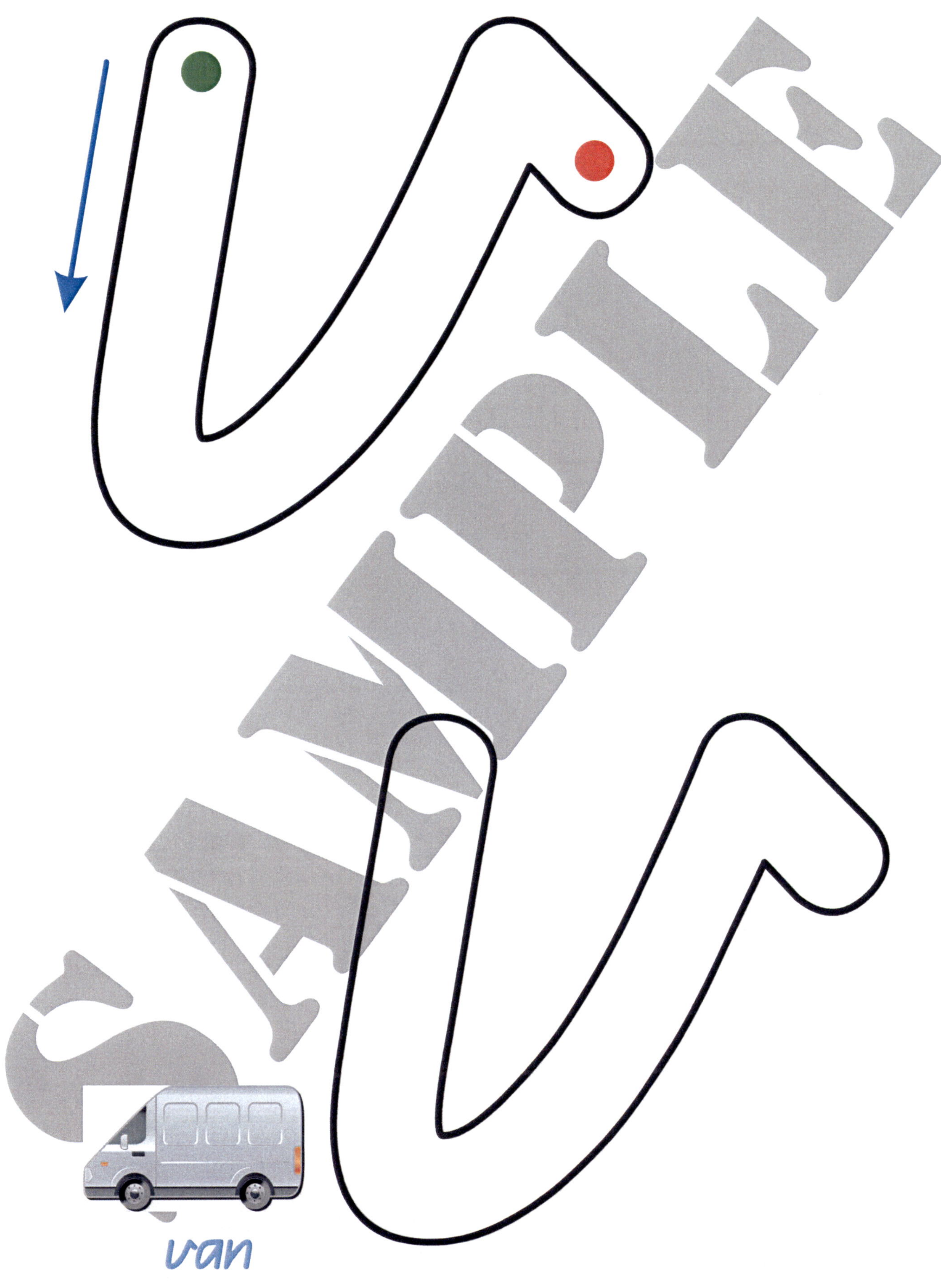
van

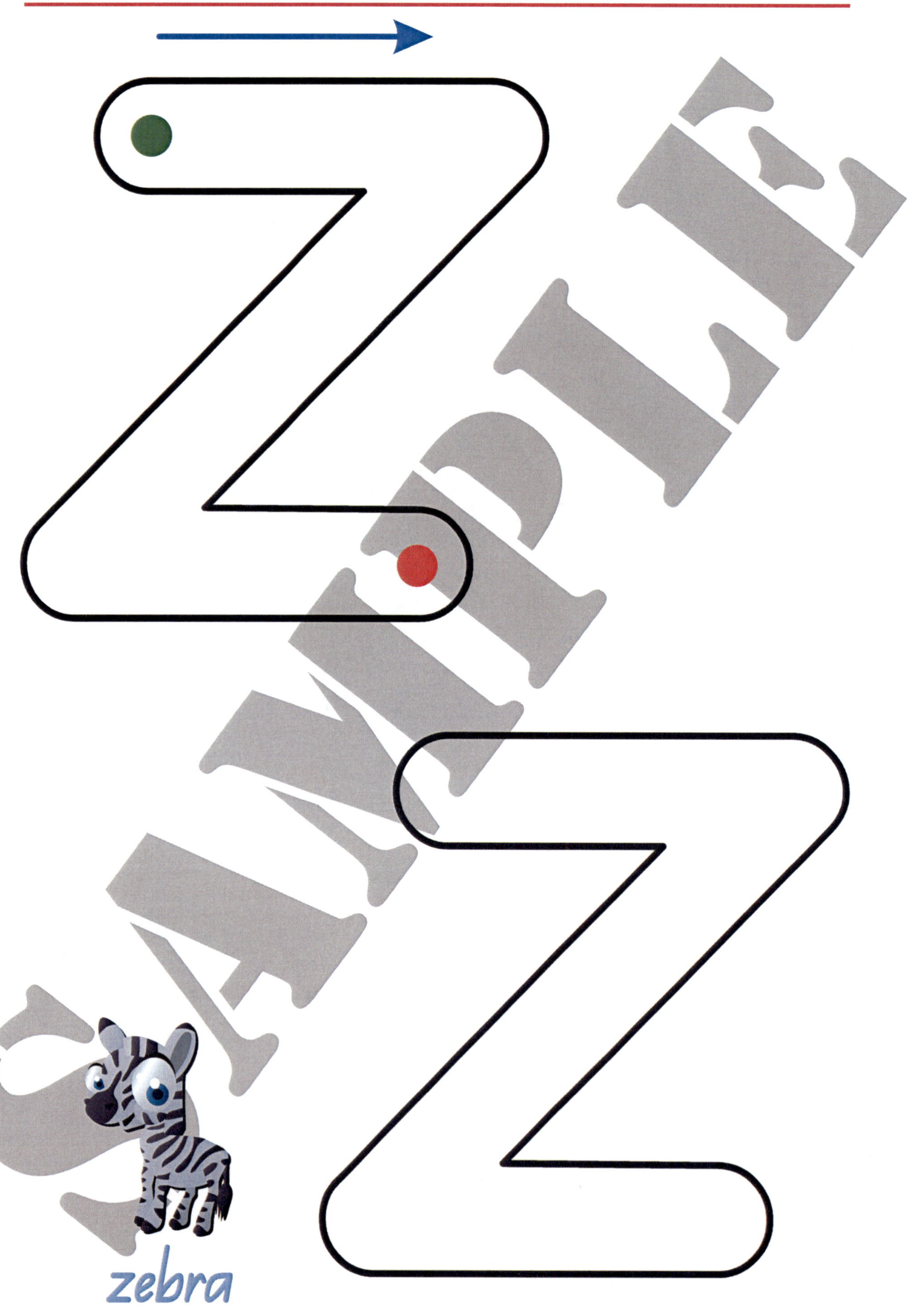
zebra

Letters on a Single Line

Blank page intentionally added.

0

a

d
d
SAMPLE

c

i
SAMPLE

t

m
m

h
h

r

b
b

p
SAMPLE

f

e

и

g
g

qu
qu
SAMPLE

w
w

x

y
y

s

v

z
SAMPLE

Multiple Letters on a Single Line

Blank page intentionally added.

o

a
ao
oa

d

da

do

ad

od

c

ca

co

ac

oc

i

ia

ai

io

did

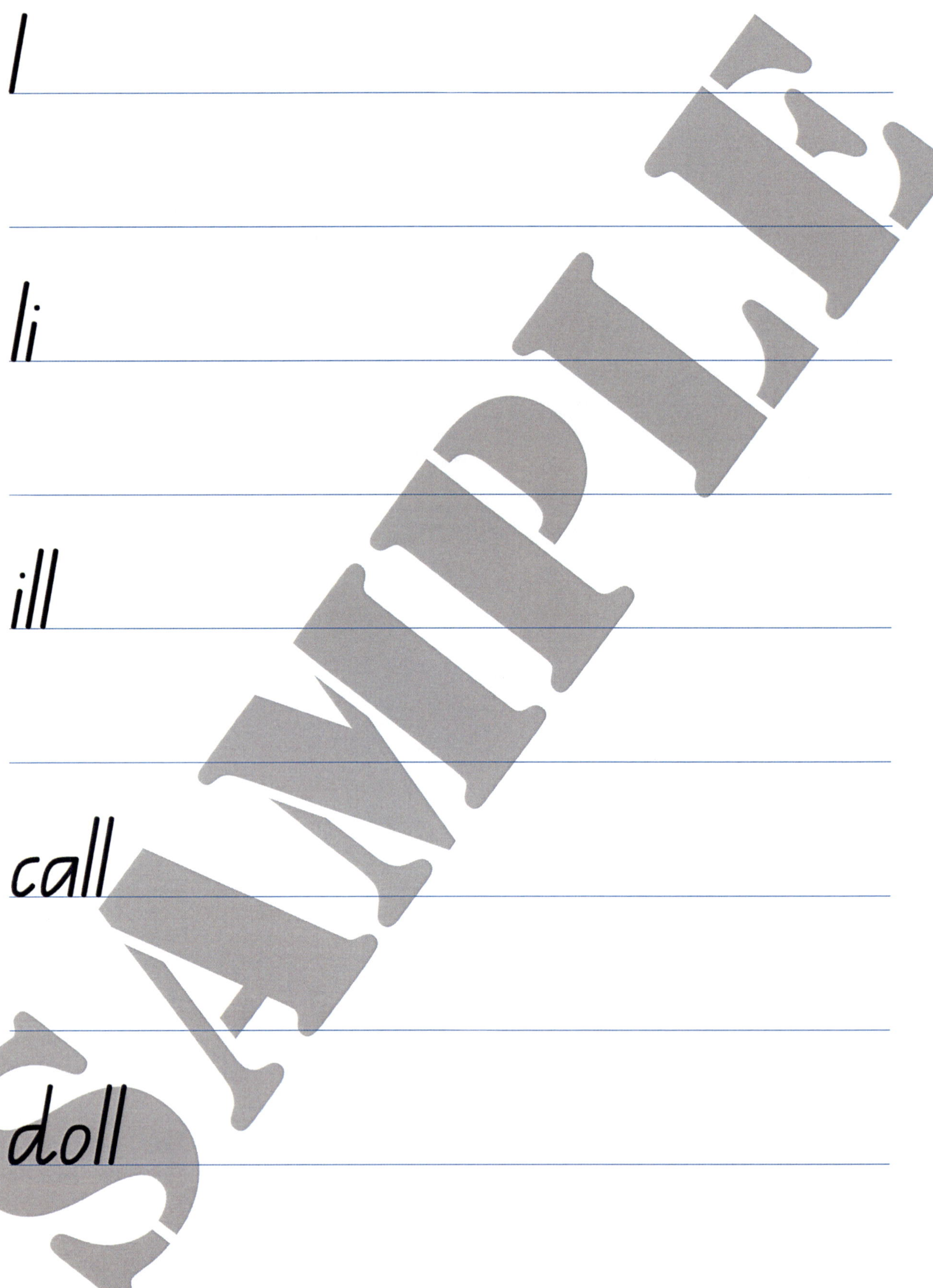

l

li

ill

call

doll

t

it

to

at

cat

dot

m

ma

om

mill

mat

n

ni

on

nod

tin

h

hi

oh

him

had

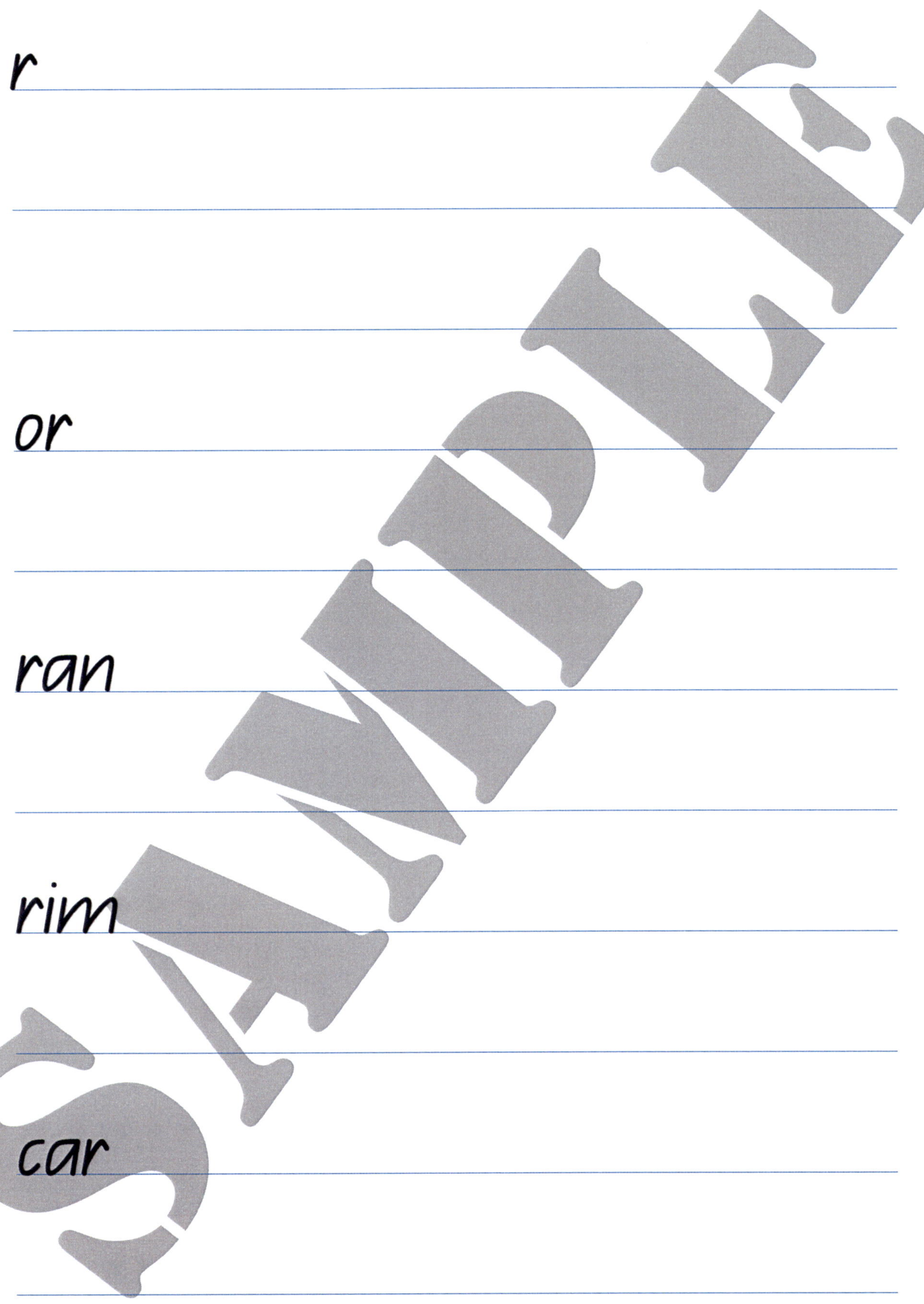

r

or

ran

rim

car

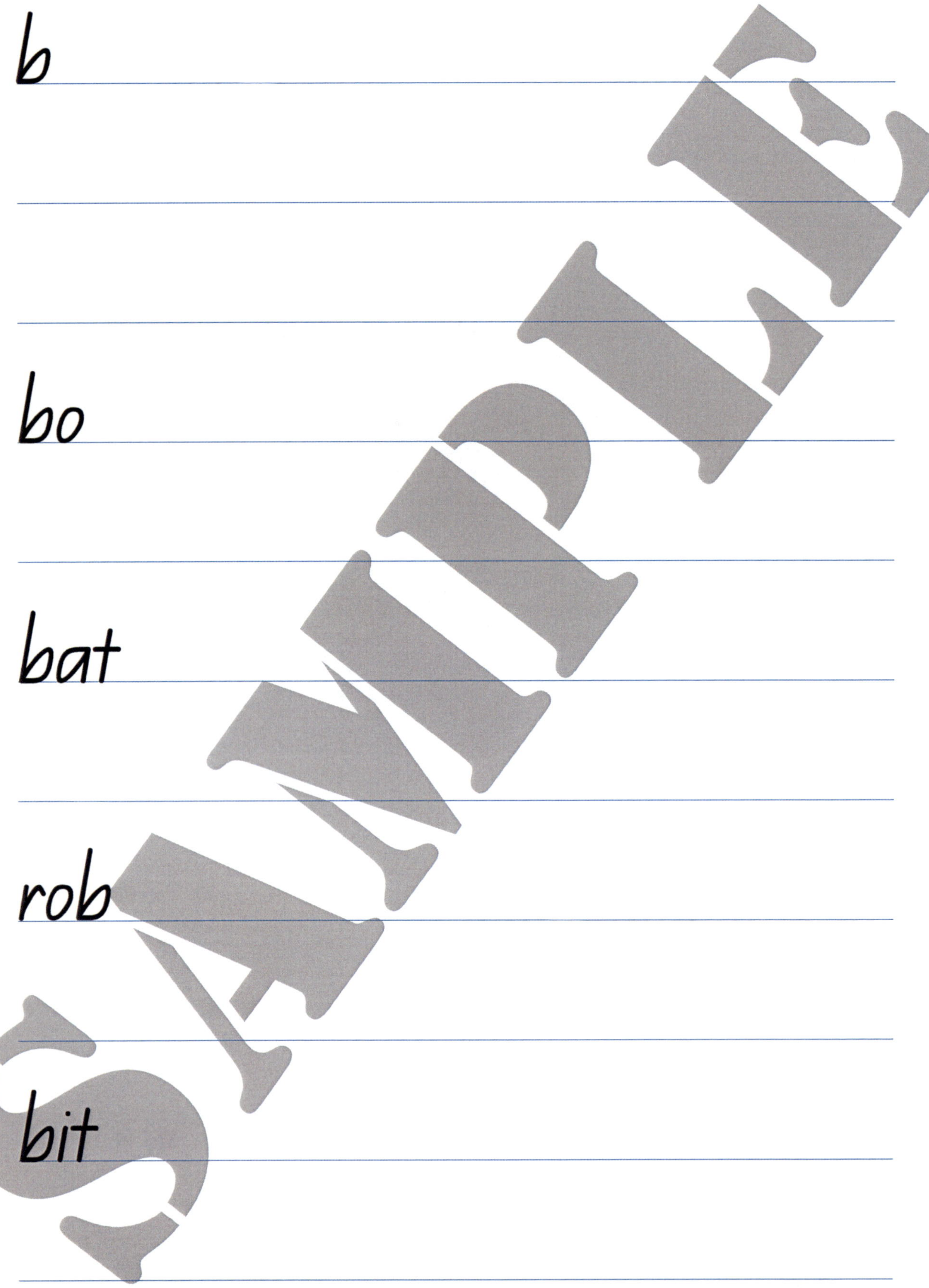

b

bo

bat

rob

bit

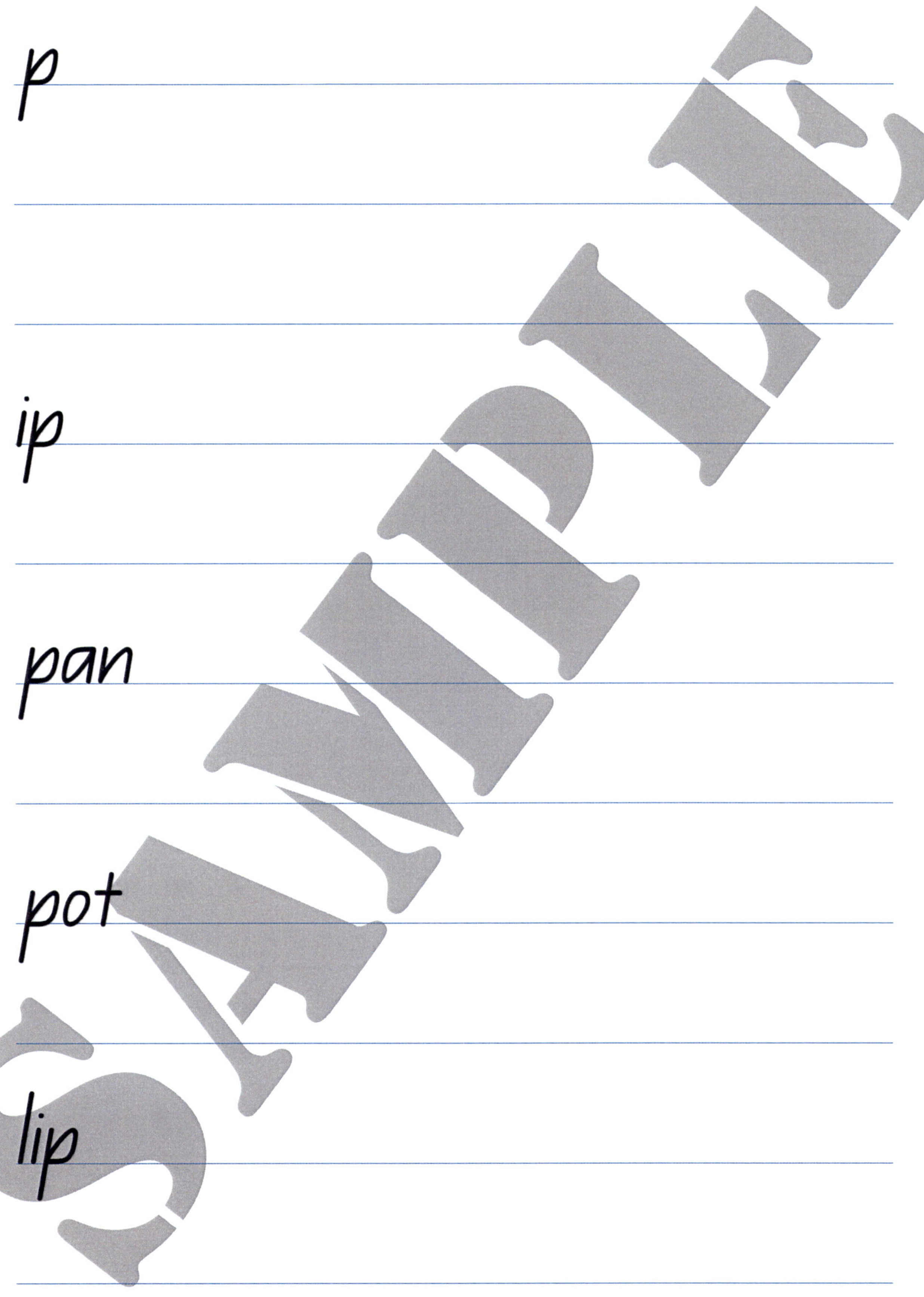

p

ip

pan

pot

lip

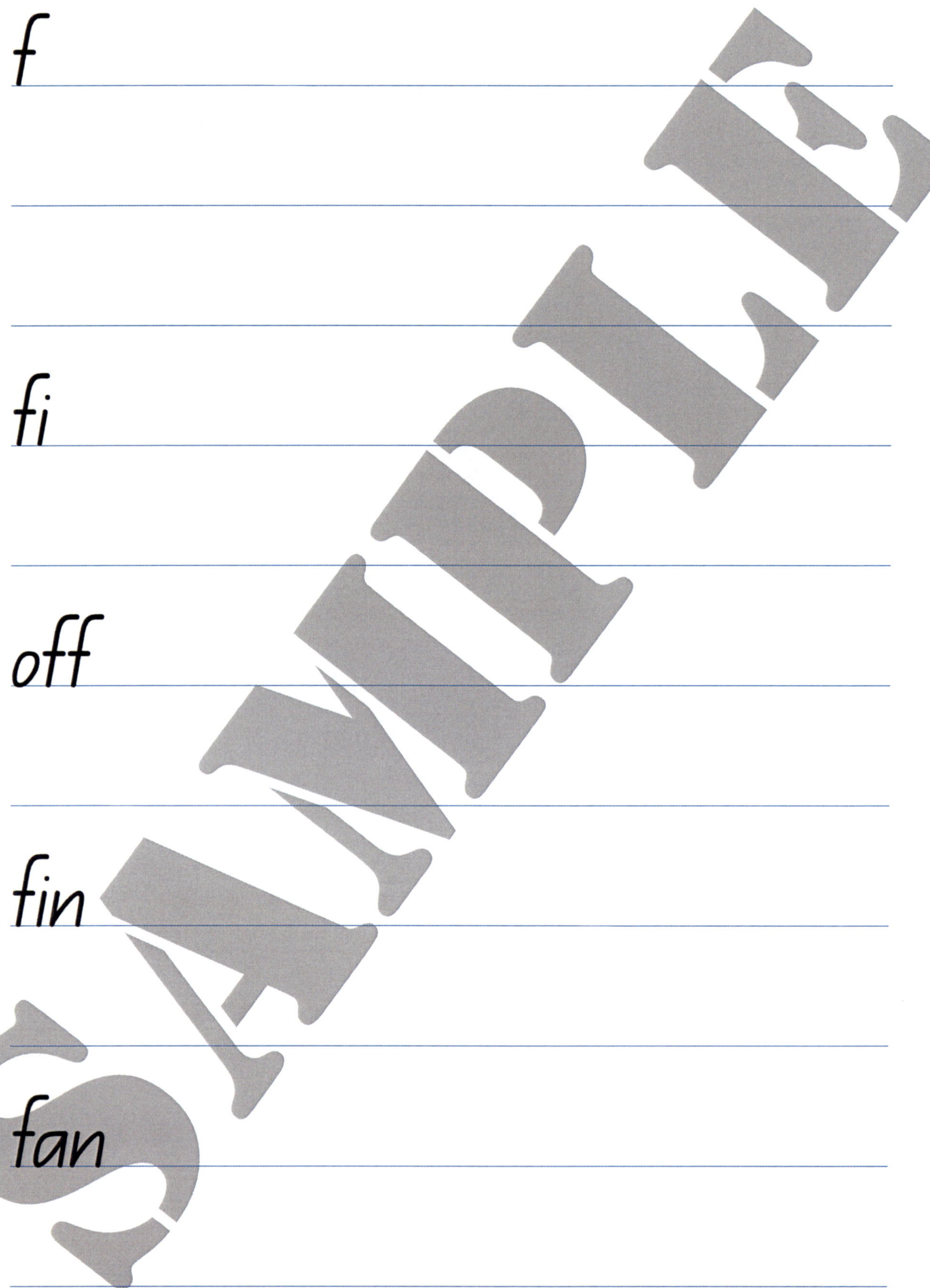

f

fi

off

fin

fan

e

ei

ae

fed

hen

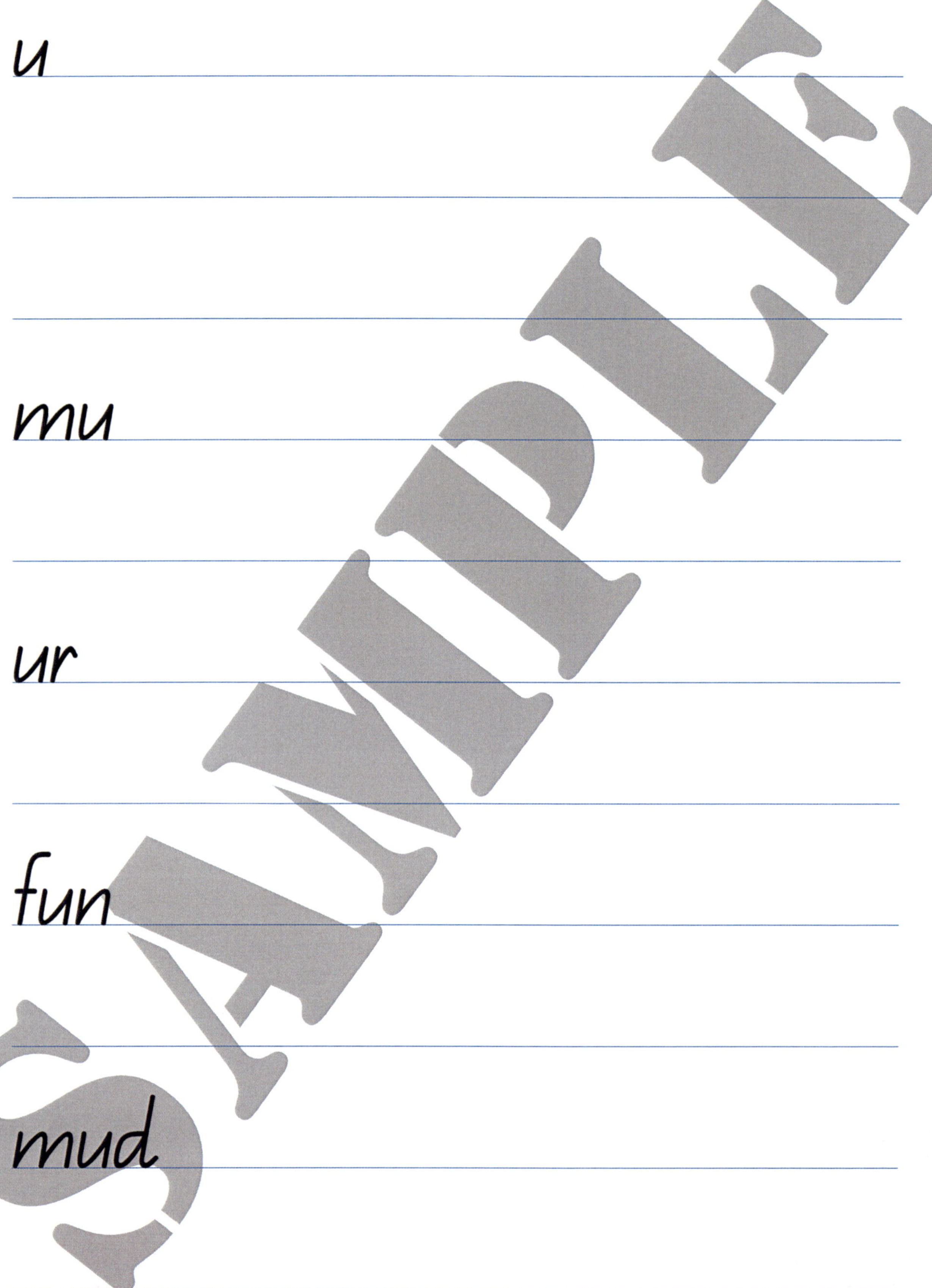

u

mu

ur

fun

mud

g

gr

ig

egg

fig

grub

j

je

jog

jam

jet

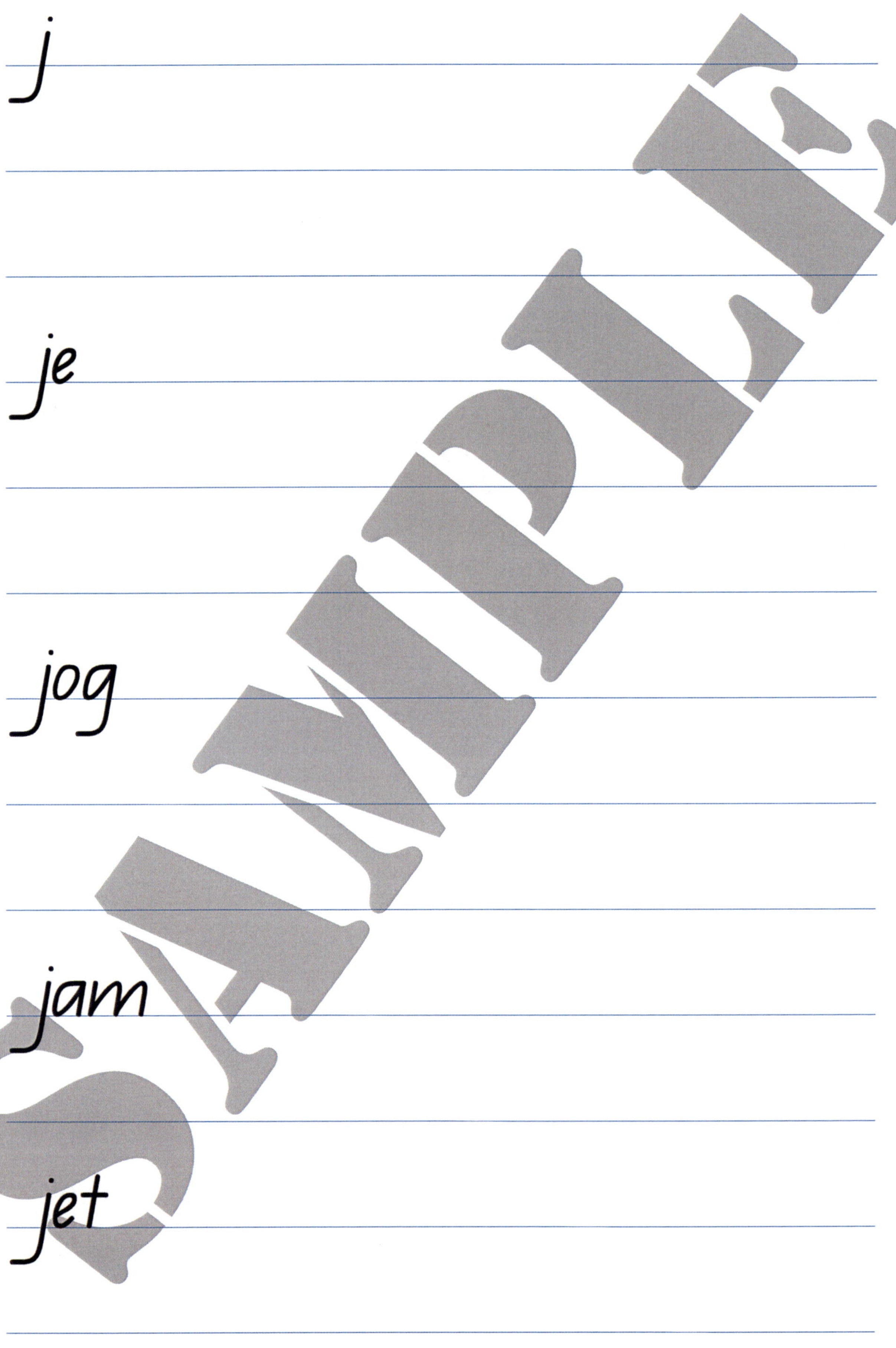

qu

que

qui

quell

queen

quoll

w

we

ew

wag

web

with

x

ex

axe

fox

box

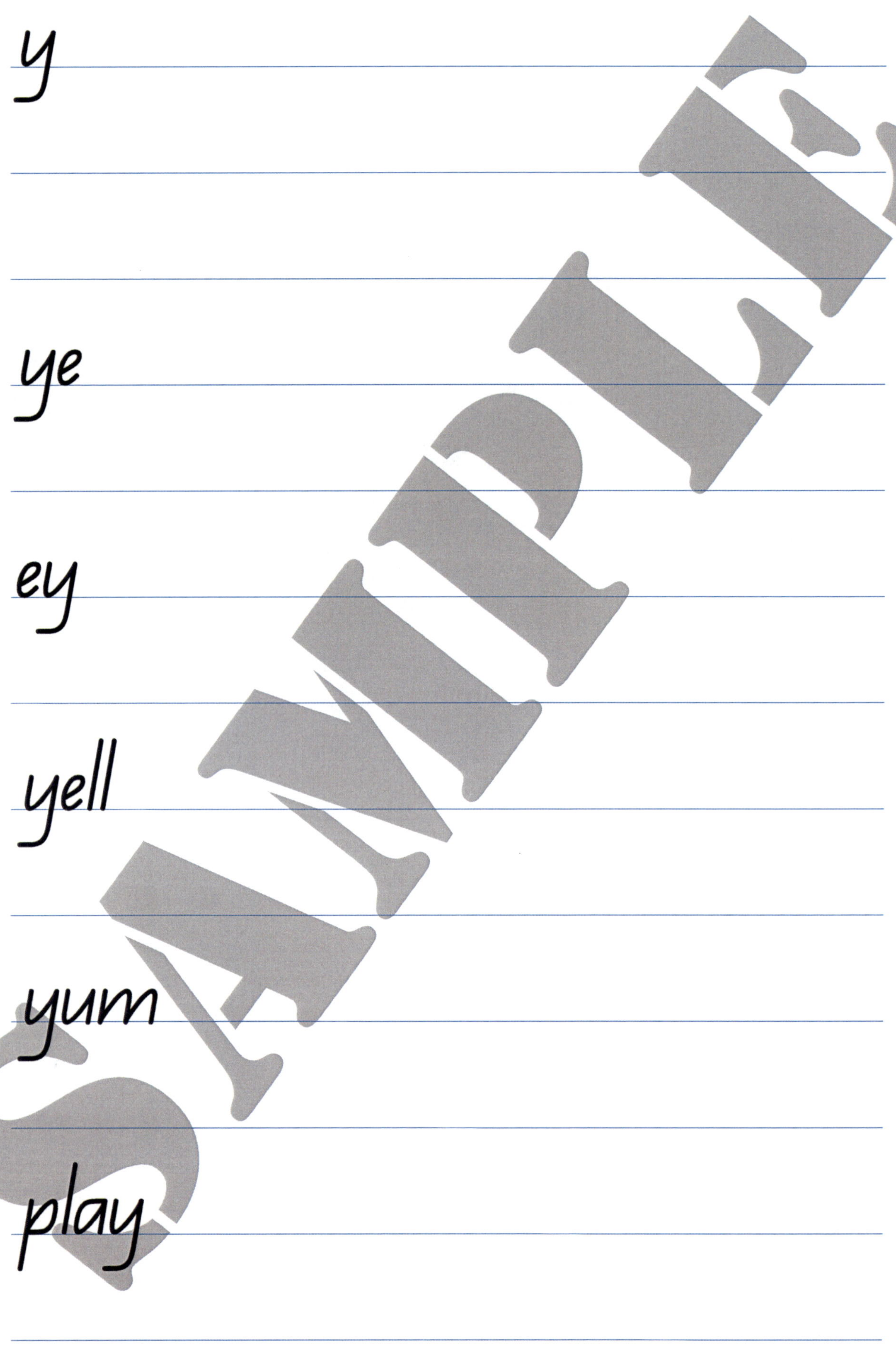

y

ye

ey

yell

yum

play

s

se

six

hiss

mess

send

k

ke

kick

luck

peck

v

ev

van

vet

vest

vote

z

zinc

zoo

zipper

zoom

zigzag

Introducing Capitals

Blank page intentionally added.

oO

o

O

Oo

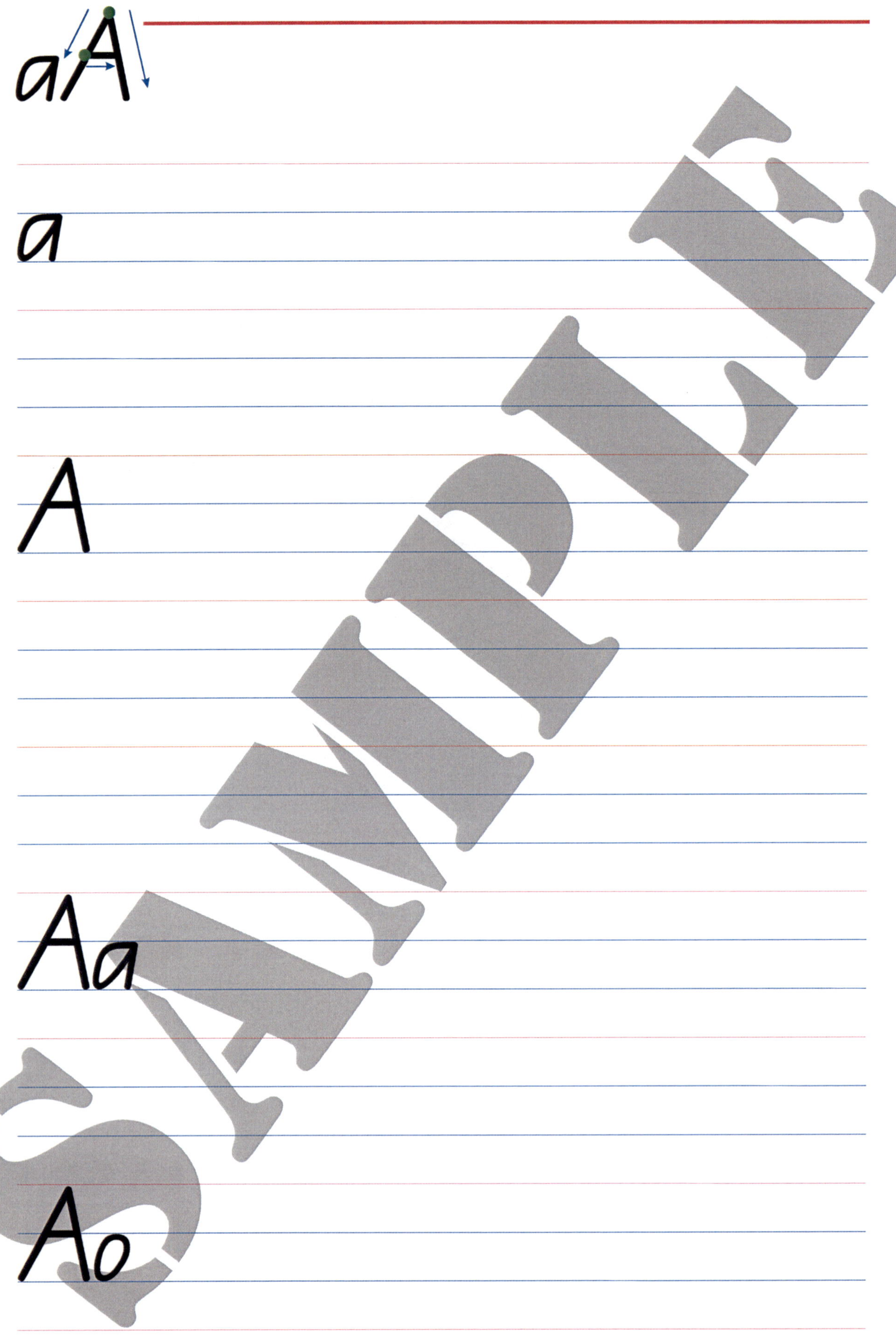
aA
a
A
Aa
Ao

dD

d

D

Dd

da

Da

Do

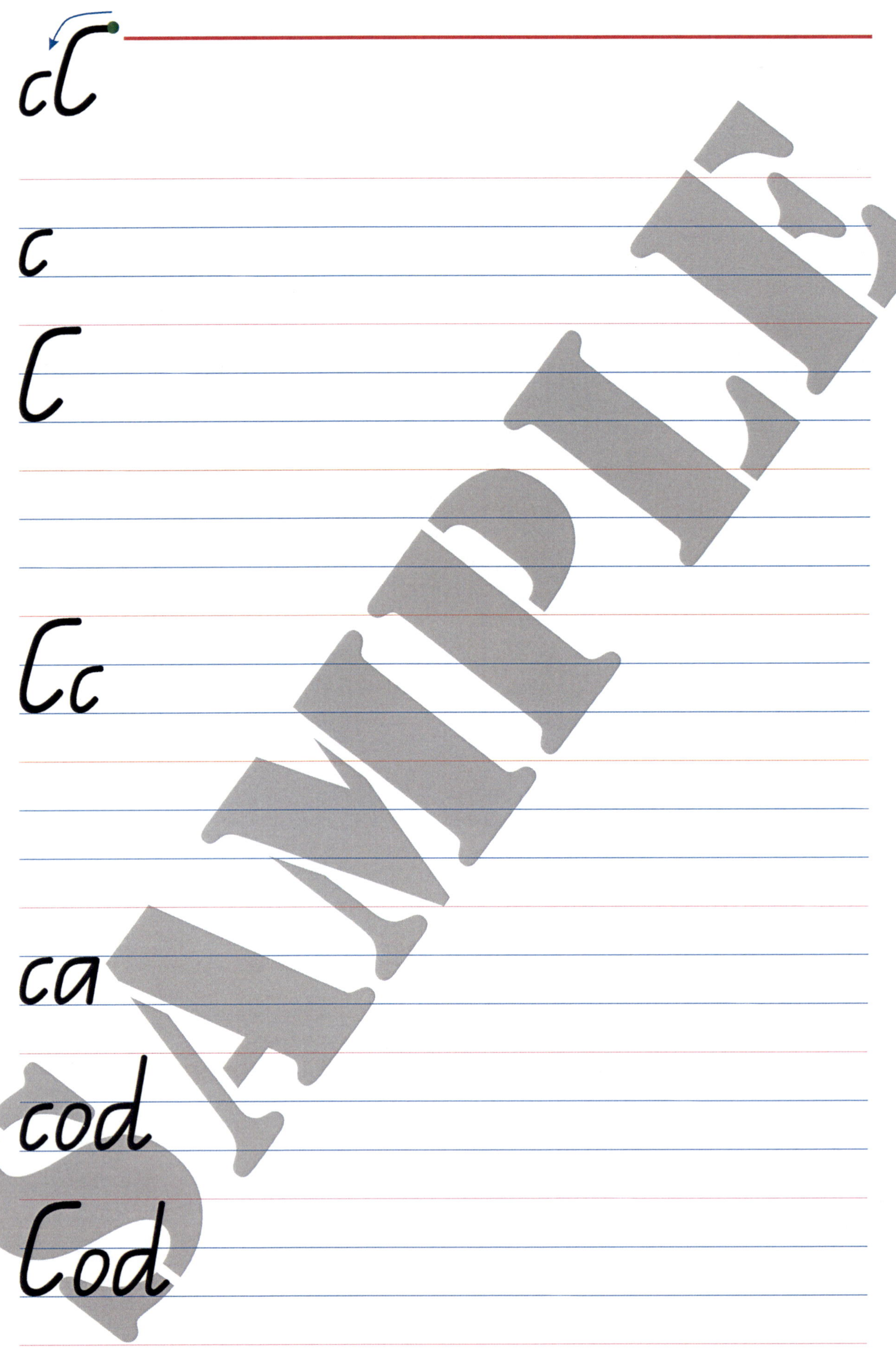

cC

c

C

Cc

ca

cod

Cod

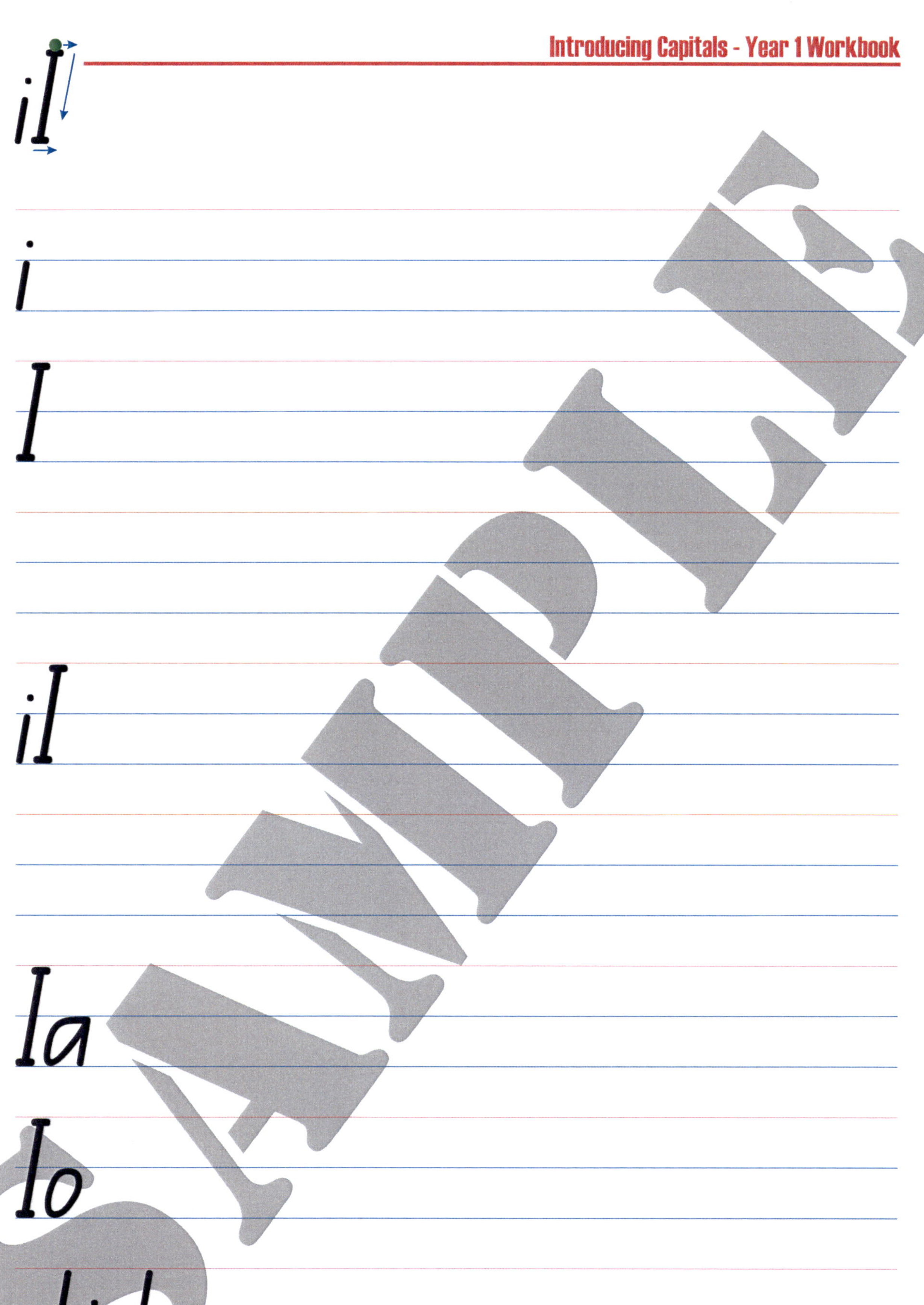

iI

i

I

iI

Ia

Io

did

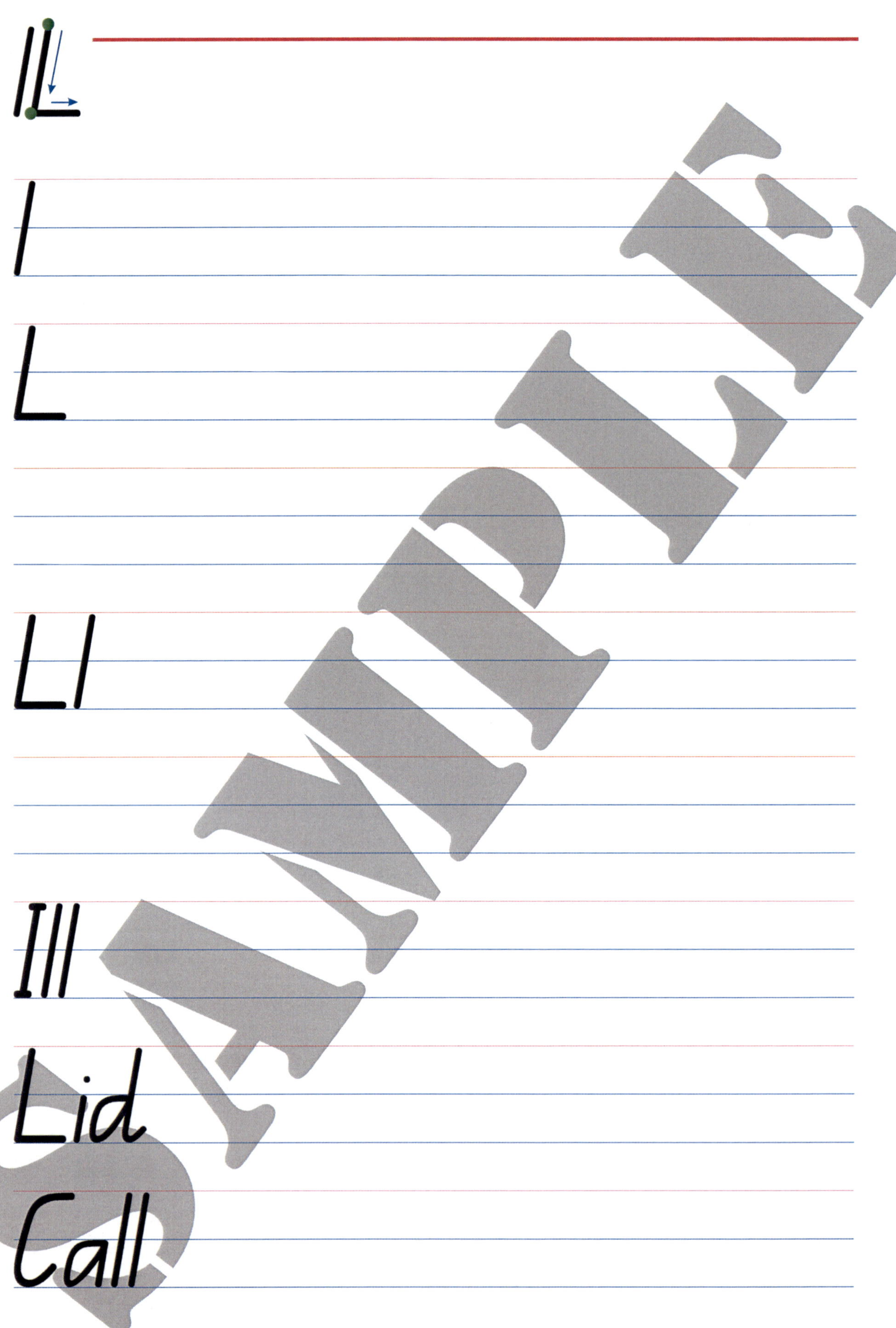

lL
l
L
Ll
Ill
Lid
Call

tT

t

T

Tt

To

Dot

Lot

Lit

cot

mM

m

M

Mm

Mat

Tim

Mill

am

Mat

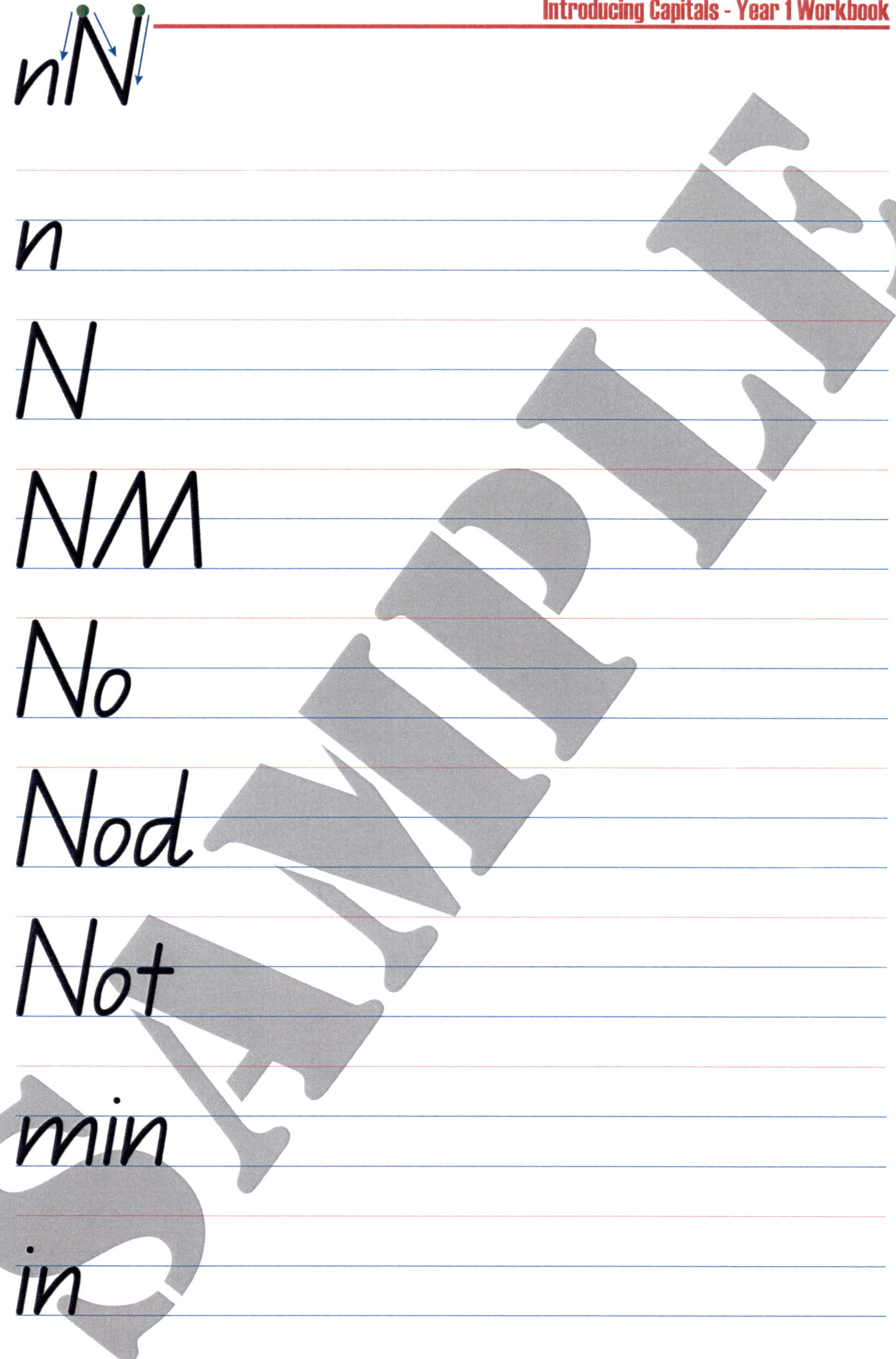

nN

n

N

NM

No

Nod

Not

min

in

hH

h

H

Hh

Hat

Hot

Him

Hall

hill

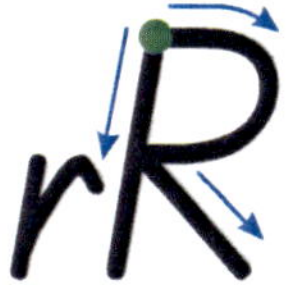

r

R

Rr

Rat

Rod

Ram

for

grin

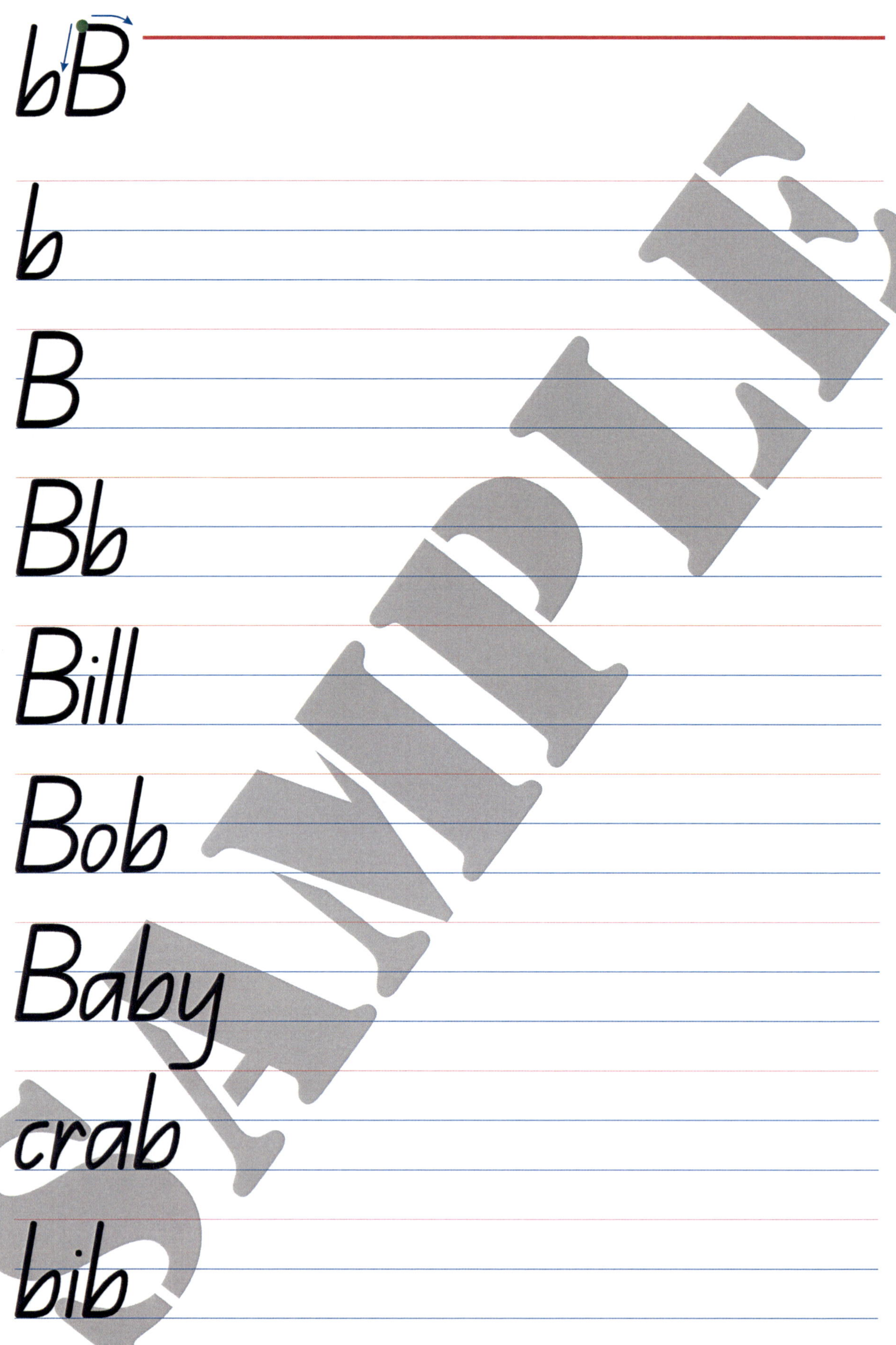

bB

b

B

Bb

Bill

Bob

Baby

crab

bib

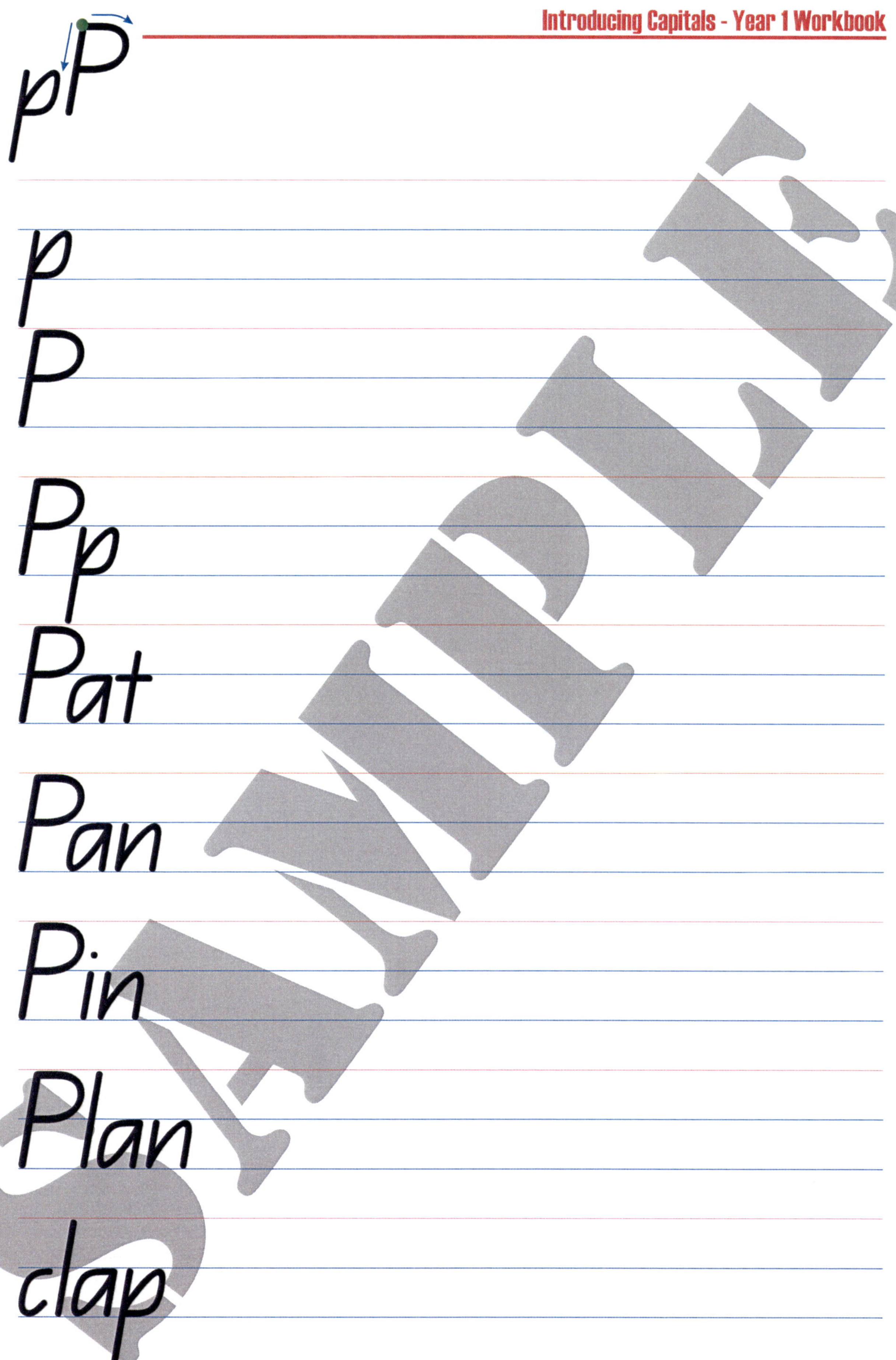

pP

p

P

Pp

Pat

Pan

Pin

Plan

clap

fF

f

F

Ff

Fran

Flag

frog

fig

from

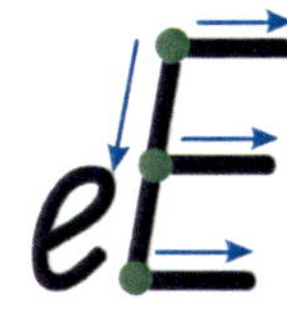

e

E

Ee

Egg

Eel

Elf

men

pen

uU

u

U

Uu

Up

Under

Uphill

run

fun

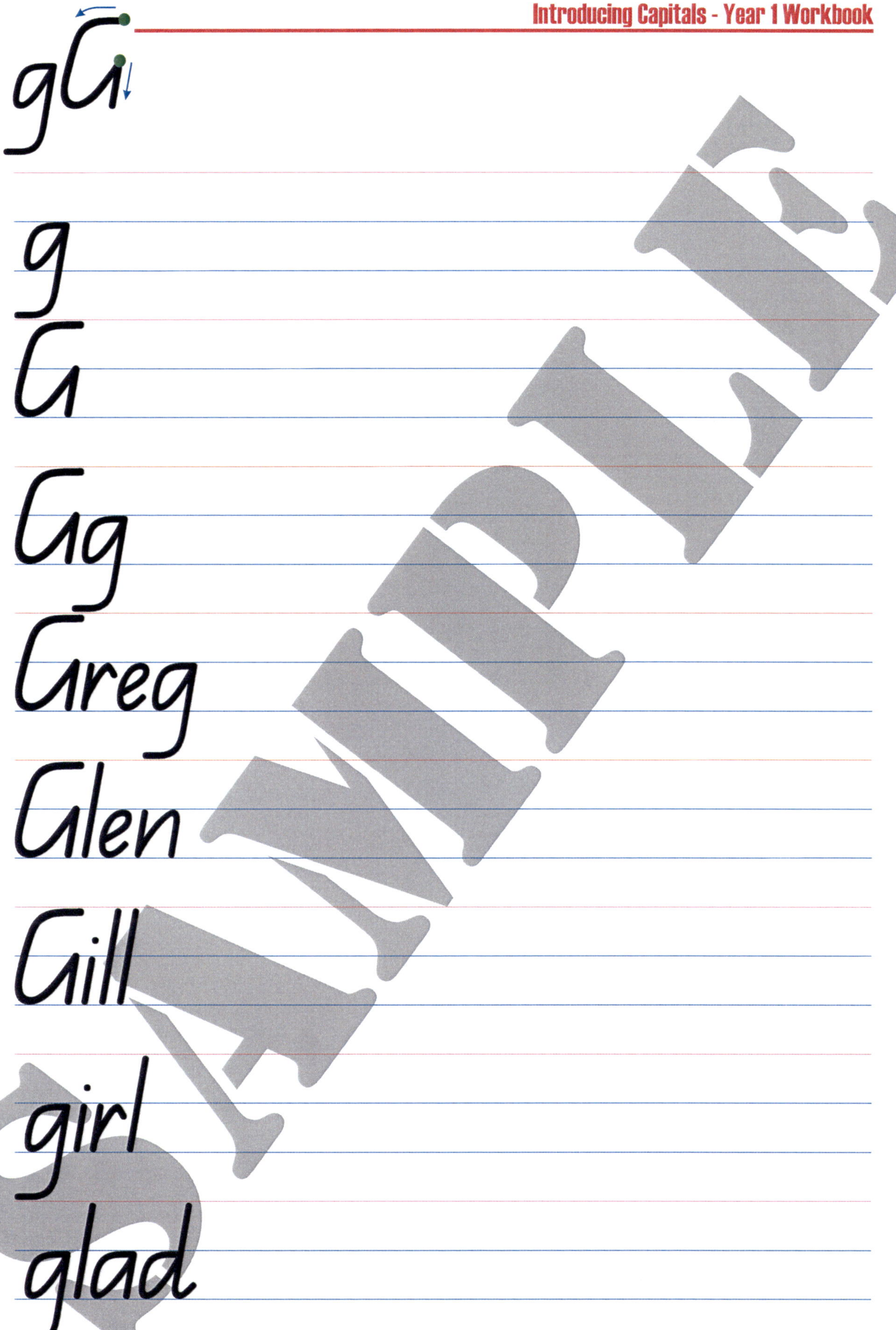
gG
g
G
Gg
Greg
Glen
Gill
girl
glad
SAMPLE

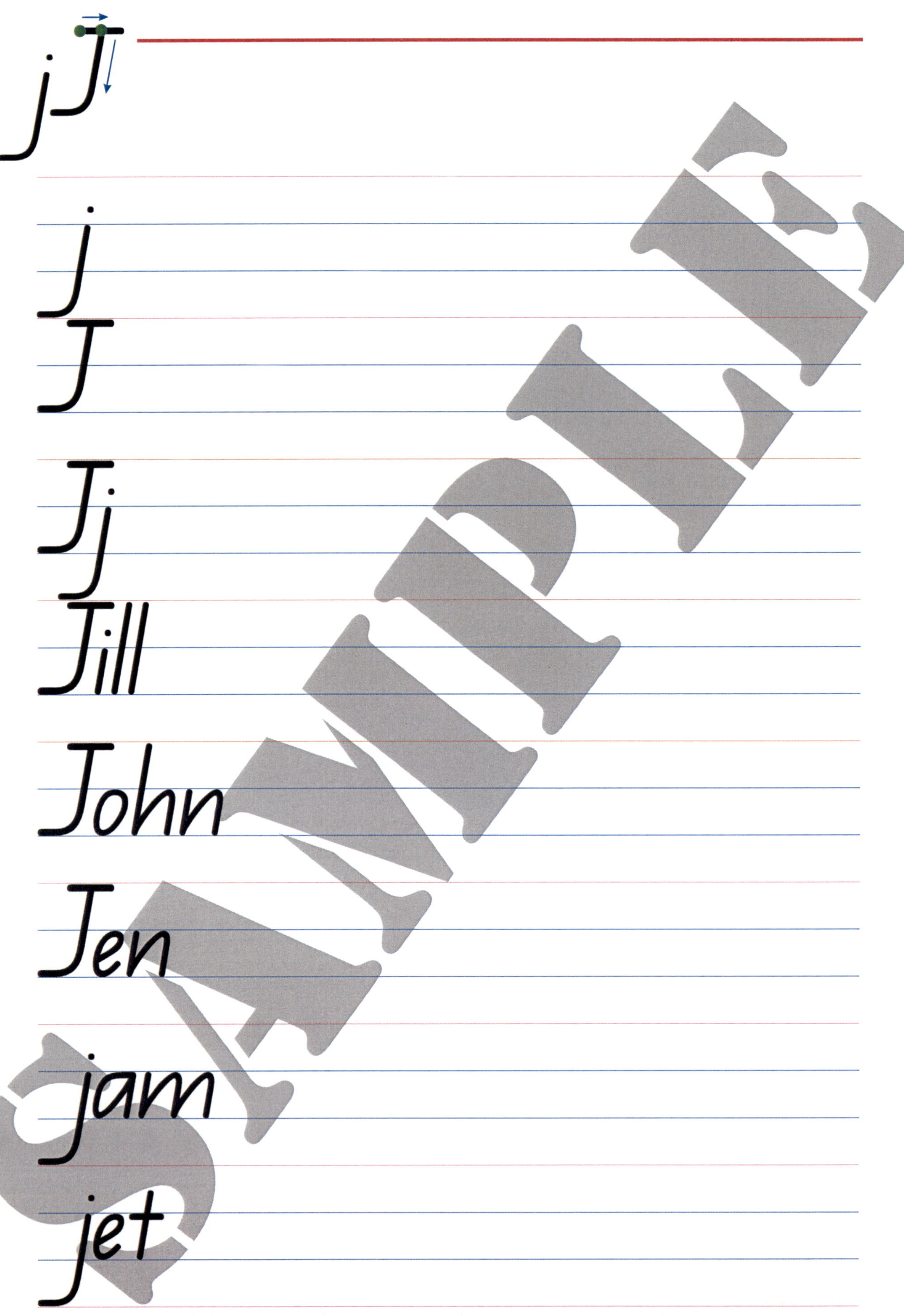

jJ

j

J

Jj

Jill

John

Jen

jam

jet

quQu

qu

Qu

Ququ

Quinn

Queen

quoll

quill

quail

w W

w

W

Ww

Walt

William

web

wind

wing

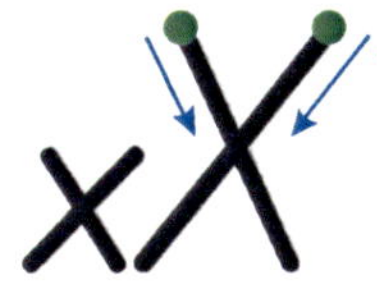

x

X

Xx

Xena

Xander

ox

fox

box

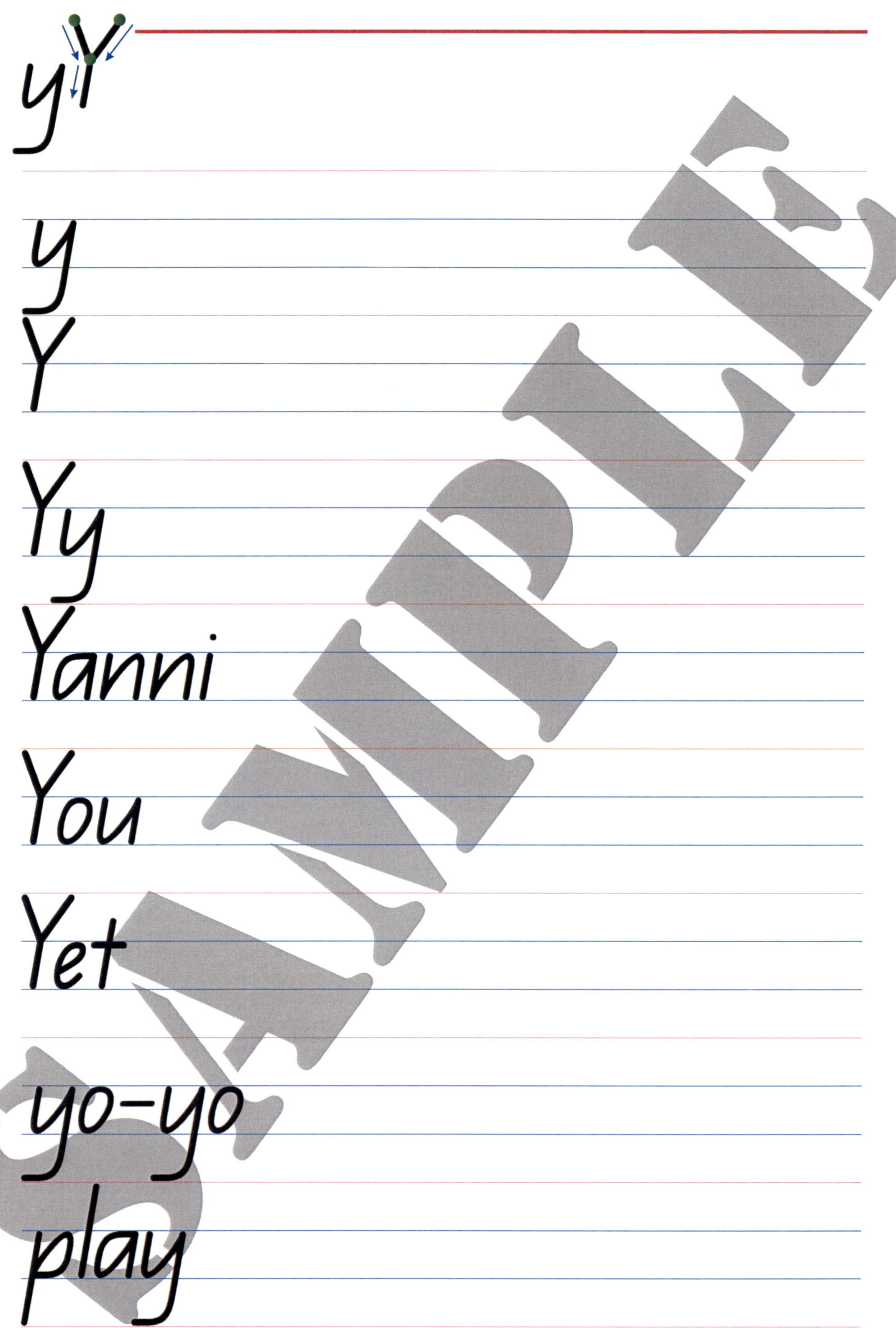
yY
y
Y
Yy
Yanni
You
Yet
yo-yo
play

s S

s

S

Ss

Susan

Sandi

bus

mess

Susan likes busses.

kK

k

K

Kk

Karen

Kay

Katrina

Black

Kevin is kind to Kate.

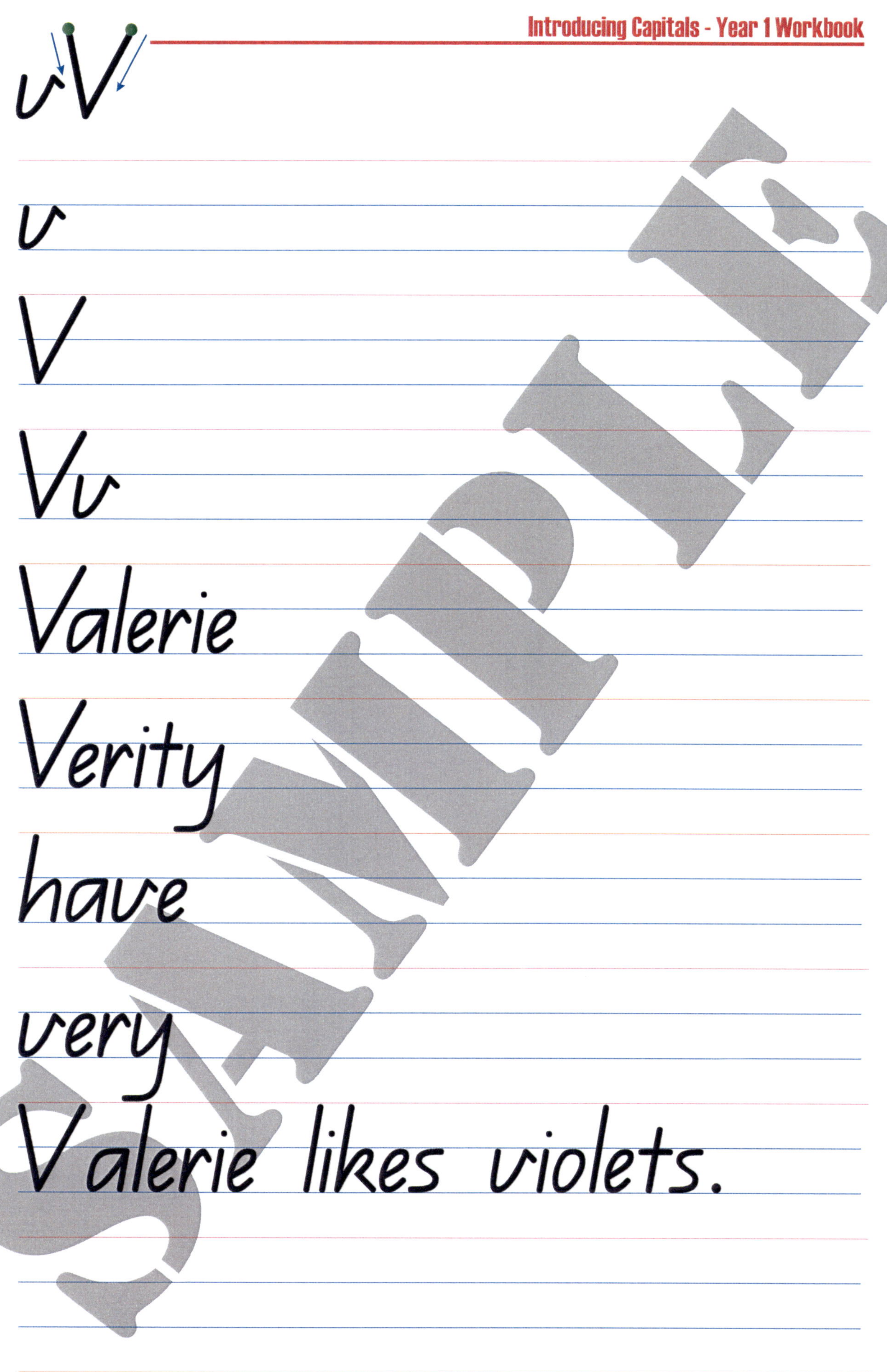

v V

v

V

Vv

Valerie

Verity

have

very

Valerie likes violets.

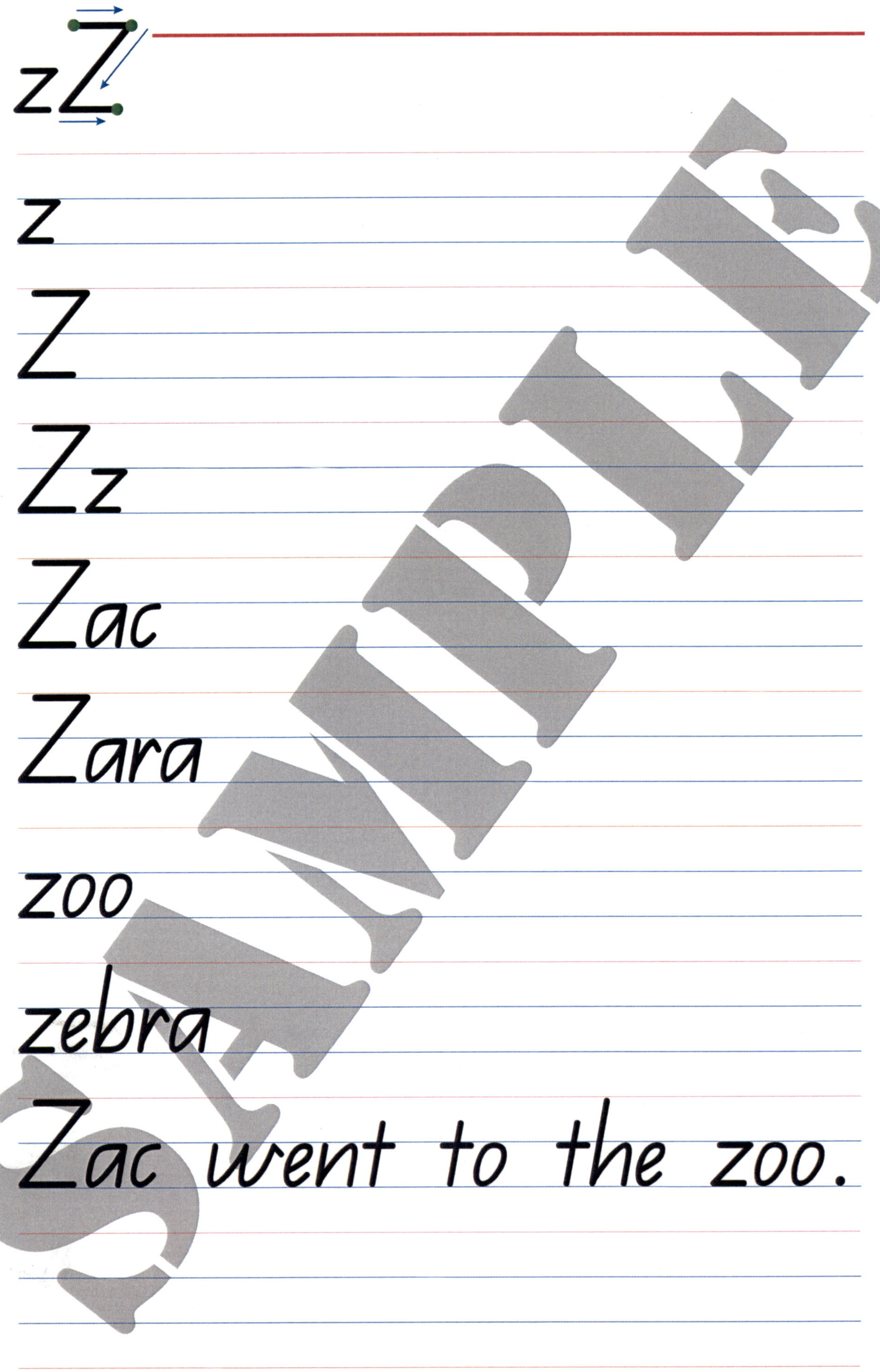

zZ

z

Z

Zz

Zac

Zara

zoo

zebra

Zac went to the zoo.